Hamlyn all-colour paperbacks

Clive Gammon

Sea Fishing

illustrated by Peter Morter
& Design Bureau

Paul Hamlyn · London
Sun Books · Melbourne

FOREWORD

Sea fishing with rod and line grows more and more popular every day. To some it offers a welcome escape from daily routine, or from indoor life to the open air, and like many other sports it gives plenty of scope for knowledge, thought and judgment. This book is an excellent introduction for the beginner who wants to know what species there are, where to look for them, and how to catch them, and it has much to offer the more experienced angler.

The book is mostly about the British Isles, though it also mentions certain specialized types of fishing in Spain and Portugal, in the Mediterranean and Scandinavia, even in the Caribbean and Pacific.

The characteristics of piers, beaches of different kinds, and other fishing-grounds are stated. The author gives a lucid explanation of what pinnacle rock and other types of rock offer the angler.

Fish of different species are discussed in detail, and in special sections where appropriate. Whether he is describing typical surroundings or particular species and their ways, the author is always providing a digest of factual information and practical guidance.

There are explanations of how to pick up pinnacle rock and other marks for offshore fishing.

The author deals in detail with the thrilling and popular sport of big-game fishing, and gives a wealth of advice on fishing for big fish of many species.

The text throughout is illustrated in full colour with lifelike pictures of fish, of equipment, and of fishing methods and surroundings.

Published by The Hamlyn Publishing Group Limited
London · New York · Sydney · Toronto
Hamlyn House, Feltham, Middlesex, England
In association with Sun Books Pty Ltd Melbourne

Phototypeset by Oliver Burridge Filmsetting Limited, Crawley, Sussex
Colour separations by Schwitter Limited, Zurich
Printed in England by Sir Joseph Causton & Sons Limited

CONTENTS

PIER FISHING

It is safe to say that most sea anglers begin by fishing from piers. There are many good reasons for this. A pier gives them access to deeper water than they can expect to reach by casting from the shore – and, to the novice especially, this seems to be a clear-cut advantage. Moreover, pier fishing is physically easier – no rock-scrambling, a handy place to prop a rod, and shelter when it rains. A Sunday morning spent on the pier is something of a social occasion also – other anglers to talk to, and to share the disappointment when catches are meagre!

It must be confessed that pier fishing rarely provides the best sport, though this comment must be qualified by recalling

Under the pier – fishing close to the water.

Amongst the piles barnacles, mussels and weed attract small bait-fish — food for big predators.

that there are exceptions. Deal pier can be magnificent for winter cod; Fenit pier in Ireland has yielded skate of more than a hundred pounds. However, pier fishing does provide an undemanding introduction to the sport, and even small whiting and flatfish, the usual catch, are exciting enough when they are the first sea fish that the angler has ever taken home.

But by thinking like a fish (always a good rule!) you can put up a better performance than the majority of pier fishermen do. Ask yourself what there is about a pier that attracts fish, and where, in relation to the pier, they are likely to be found.

Look first at the construction of the pier itself, and note how the sea has affected it below the high-tide mark. A low-tide inspection from a dinghy will reveal that the piles are well encrusted with weed and marine creatures like barnacles and mussels. These, in themselves, have little attraction for fair-sized fish (except mullet), but they do attract small bait fish, which in turn provide feed for big predators. And the latter – bass, for example – know that ambushes are possible amongst the shadowy piles. Moreover, a pier that stands on piles has more than one level, so that when circumstances allow the fish are accessible from this as well as from the greater height of the upper deck.

All in all, a pier offers a fair amount of scope.

Float-fishing from a pier.

Methods and Techniques

From thoughtful inspection of a typical pier, one can gather that long-casting from piers is often a mistake. It is much better to fish as closely as possible to the pier itself. Unfortunately – and this is one of the basic drawbacks of pier fishing – there is usually a lot of overcrowding. But you can fish in the early morning – or through the night where this is allowed.

One of the most effective pier-fishing methods is float fishing. In the early morning especially, quite large bass and pollack may visit the pier, and a float worked amongst the piles, with sand eel, ragworm or small live fish for bait, can account for good fish. Tackle must be stout: holding fish of ten pounds – not an unreasonable expectation – from a mass of ironwork necessitates this. A short boat-rod, with a single-action reel loaded with fifteen pounds (breaking strain) mono-filament is perfect if you can fish close to the water from the lower deck of the pier. If you fish from a vantage point high above the water, a beach-casting rod will be better, as it will give you more control.

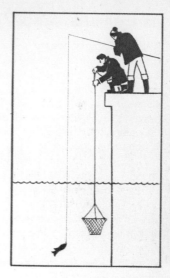

Using a drop-net.

From the higher level you will need a drop-net for fish of any size. (Never, never try hauling a big fish up the side of a pier. The line, or your rod-top, will break.) On some piers drop-nets are provided by a beneficent local authority. On others you must supply your own.

Mullet provide splendid sport for the pier float-fisherman at times – but these fish are not to be caught when holiday crowds are about! Much finer tackle is needed, too, though the fish are big and strong.

Mackerel and garfish are other possibilities for the float-fishing method. Here there must be an exception to the rule, and the float tackle must be streamed away on the tide.

Spinning will take mackerel, pollack and bass, but here again you need room to cast, and a platform close to the water.

Bottom fishing with a natural bait comes into its own in the autumn and winter, with the arrival of cod and whiting shoals. Lugworm, sprat or herring are suitable baits to be fished in the tidal currents.

FISH OF THE SANDBANKS

To the sea angler, the turbot is one of the most desirable fish, not so much for its sporting qualities (close to nil) but because it is such a prize to take home. Turbot is highly esteemed for the table. It may reach thirty pounds or more. The turbot is diamond-shaped. The body is without scales, but on the same side as the eyes there are small tubercles (bony protruberances). This side is usually grey or brown, and speckled; the other side of the turbot is white.

The chief problem in catching turbot lies in finding them, for as a result of intensive trawling they are a somewhat localized species in the waters around the British Isles. Some marks (positions), because the physical configuration of the bottom makes it impossible to work a trawl, are well known to British sea anglers, many of whom make special trips to fish them. Most famous is the Skerries, off Dartmouth, but the Varne Bank, in the narrows of the English Channel, and the Shambles Bank, off Weymouth, both have a high reputation.

Turbot not only run big, but make delicious eating.

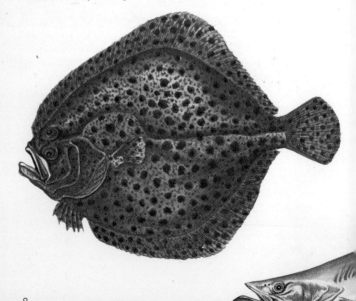

All these marks have a feature in common: they are sand-banks rising quite suddenly out of deep water. Turbot frequent them because they hold a considerable store of greater sand eels. (Although we do not usually think of flatfish as predators, the turbot is almost exclusively a fish-eater.) A quick look at a turbot will reveal that it is not built for speed. Instead, it uses the configuration of the sandbank to lie in wait for sand eels and other small fish that are brought towards it by the force of the tide.

Notice also the turbot's mouth, which provides an excellent clue as to how it feeds and takes a bait. The mouth is telescopic, and extends like a vacuum cleaner to suck in its prey. This accounts for the typical turbot bite – by no means a tearaway rush, but a slow, solid take. Remember that no one ever lost a turbot by giving it too much time. If you feel a turbot hit, wait for a second knock, then cautiously tighten up until you feel the weight of the fish. Time will not be wasted in waiting for the right moment.

Catching a turbot calls for judgement and care, but these are well worth while for so prized a fish.

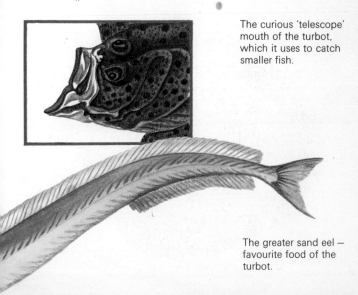

The curious 'telescope' mouth of the turbot, which it uses to catch smaller fish.

The greater sand eel — favourite food of the turbot.

Tackle for Turbot

The tackle to use varies greatly with the surroundings in which the turbot are found. I have caught turbot in shallow, almost tideless, water in the West of Ireland on a spinning rod, and using only an ounce of lead. On the other hand, I have found them in places where the circumstances require very different techniques. Since most turbot fishing involves a boat-fishing visit to one of the recognized marks I have mentioned, the standard tackle for these places should be described here.

A standard, hollow glass boat-rod around seven feet long with a five-pound test curve should be matched with a big, single-action reel or a multiplier around size 4/0. Although some specialist turbot fishermen use a fifty-pound b.s. line, there is no need to go heavier than thirty-five pounds. The main task of the tackle is to haul quite a heavy fish that puts up a considerable resistance to the tide because of its shape – but it *is* no more than hauling work. You need expect no heart-stopping runs or frantic sounding for the bottom. Indeed, on a number of occasions I have stopped hauling for a short rest, in the confident knowledge that the turbot would rest with me until it was time to get him on the move again.

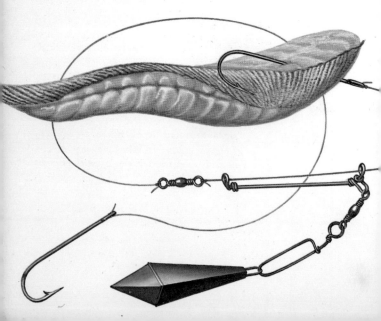

The best end tackle to use is a long, flowing trace – as long, in fact, as you can conveniently manage. This can be the same monofilament nylon that you use for your line. At the business end is your hook – if it is big turbot you are after, it should not be less than 6/0, and well-sharpened – and at the other a swivel which stops a Clements boom, on to which is clipped the weight. The size of this will depend upon the run of tide you encounter – often a considerable one on such a mark as the Skerries, where strong currents among the rocks at various stages of the tide necessitate an adequate weight.

Bait is a long lask of mackerel, or a whole fillet from the side of a sand eel. Why a fillet should be more killing than the sand eel used whole is difficult to say, but it is an undeniable fact. In this case the only explanation that can be given is that it is just one of the things to be learned by practical experience. It should be mounted so that it flows in the tide in as natural a way as possible.

It will then have a good chance of attracting a turbot cruising in search of his favourite food.

(*Left*) Tackle with a piece of fish as bait. (*Above*) A standard hollow-glass boat-rod and single reel for turbot.

Plaice

(*Right*) A mussel bed is attractive to plaice.

Where to Find Plaice

Plaice, of course, are flatfish. On the same side as the eyes the fish is brownish-green with orange spots, not very close together. The other side is white. Very large plaice may run up to about ten pounds or more. The fish is highly esteemed for the table, and provides good sport.

Recently plaice have increased considerably in numbers in British coastal waters, and fears that intensive trawling had practically removed them from the angling picture have proved to be unfounded. Naturally, trawling still goes on, but there are plenty of spots where many plaice can be caught. In a recent summer, for example, enormous catches of plaice were made in the neighbourhood of Rye Bay. But plaice are of general distribution all around the coasts of the British Isles, and the Rye Bay fish attracted attention simply because of the very large number of anglers who fished them.

Plaice are fish of sandy grounds – banks and inshore bays. They come inshore in April, and the fishing remains good until

the winter, when they make their spawning migration to deeper waters. They may go down as far as eighty fathoms.

What the inshore angler has to bear in mind is that feature-less sand has much less attraction for plaice than that which holds a good supply of their natural food – chiefly shellfish but with some marine worms. The mouth of the plaice is so constructed that it can chip or crush the shell and get at the fish inside.

Thus, a bed of mussels, a large colony of cockles or razor-fish (which are of course shellfish), or areas where lugworms are likely to be washed from the sand, are all points that will draw plaice in large numbers.

Here they can feed happily enough, and although they are not predatory in the same sense as fast, voracious fish that attack other fish with speed and fury, they are yet often capable of providing the angler with quite lively sport.

Now let us consider some of the methods by which the fisherman with rod and line can catch plaice, and the tech-niques that experience has shown to be rewarding.

Tackle and Techniques for Plaice

Most fun is to be had from plaice fishing when tackle is kept really light. Unlike turbot, plaice are easily fished from a small boat close inshore, and where the easy run of tide does not dictate heavy leads and, consequently, stout rods and heavy line. Nor are the fish themselves particularly large – a seven-pounder is about the limit of any reasonable angler's ambitions. As has been said already, plaice can fight quite well in shallow water, in spite of their shape, and to get the best out of them, light tackle must be used.

For specialist plaice fishing, a trout spinning rod, with a fixed spool or single-action reel loaded with six-pound line, is perfectly adequate. With gear of this sort, very light leads will be found sufficient – bomb weights up to one ounce or very little more. The flowing trace that was recommended for turbot fishing will suit – scaled down, of course. The hook should be a long-shanked No. 4, and there is no need of a boom to take the weight.

Using the 'lift' method for plaice
1. Lower the rod until the bottom is felt
2. Raise the rod slowly
3. Reel in slowly until you are sure of your fish

Use a light trout-spinning rod for plaice.

Many plaice anglers make the mistake of fishing the bait on the bottom, and leaving it there until a plaice happens to come along. Some fish will be taken in this way, but it is not a specially adventurous method of fishing, and the bag may be small.

There is a far more effective technique, and one that produces better sport. It is based on the idea of active fishing for plaice, instead of being content to drop your bait to the bottom and wait in the hope that some obliging fish will come along. Stream the trace out on the tide, and let the line run out until the tap of the bottom is felt. The bait is left there for a moment, then the rod point is slowly raised until the angler's arm is well above shoulder height. Then it is lowered again until the bottom is felt, and the process is repeated. Almost always the plaice will take as the bait comes up from the bottom. You will feel a rattling bite, and the secret is to keep reeling slowly until it is apparent that the fish is well hooked.

Best bait is lugworm or ragworm. Other baits include mussels and shrimps. It is as well to have a landing net to hand in the boat.

Brill and Megrim

Brill are rarely fished for by intention: usually they are brought ashore as an unexpected bonus in the catch of a turbot fisherman. But they are not particularly rare, and in many cases they go unrecognized for what they are. Perhaps they are taken to be oddly-shaped turbot!

Yet there is no need for confusion. The shape is different. A turbot is diamond-shaped. The brill is oval, with sides that follow a gentle curve. There is, too, another check: to run a finger over the dark (upper) side of the fish. The brill is without the horny tubercles found on the turbot.

Brill may be greyish or brownish, or have a greenish hue. There are darker patches, as a rule with whitish spots. The underside is white. Brill make good eating.

Brill

The brill is not such a big fish as the turbot, though a fish of sixteen pounds has been taken with rod and line. Although often found over the same sort of ground as turbot, it lives in somewhat shallower water.

Like the turbot, it is almost exclusively a fish-eater, and has a marked preference for sand eels and sprats. But

marine worms and crustacea are taken as well, so that it is more likely than the turbot to be caught by shore fishermen casting into deep water.

The megrim, a smaller fish, is also a flatfish. In shape it is narrower than either turbot or brill. The colour is greyish-brown, or perhaps yellowish-brown. It is not very often taken by anglers.

Like its large relatives, the megrim is chiefly a fish-eater. It is much smaller than turbot or brill. The usual weight is two to three pounds.

Megrim

INSHORE FISHING

This is a kind of fishing that is offshore, yet can hardly be classed as deep-sea, since it takes place in comparatively shallow water of ten fathoms or less, often so near the beach that on a summer's day the cries of bathers can be distinctly heard by the fisherman.

It can be carried out from a quite small dinghy provided always that the boat is suitable, and that the person in charge knows how to handle it. This includes being able to recognize suitable and unsuitable weather and various hazards to be guarded against or avoided.

For more comfort, a quarter-decked twenty-five-footer is better. And it can be used in weather that is unsuitable for a twelve-footer.

To make the most of such fishing, the angler must be able to 'read' the coastline and the set of the tides. This ability is acquired usually by long experience (which is why the services of a good professional fisherman are worth paying for), but

Some of the details shown on a chart. Wavy lines = a tide-race; 'Kn' = Knots; 'Sp' = 'Springs' (highest tide); 'Np' = 'neaps' (lowest tide).

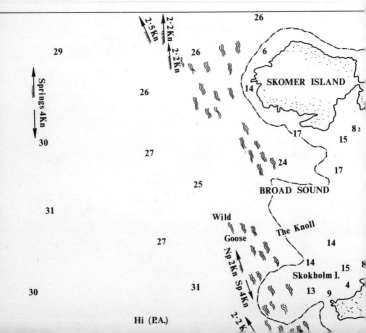

(*Above*) Where the current runs
strongly: a tide-run.

(*Below*) This stoutly-built
twenty-footer is used for fishing.

the intelligent angler can call on another ally as well – an
Admiralty Chart of the area he is going to fish. These charts
(obtainable from the authorized Agents) give depths and tides,
the nature of the bottom and the location of reefs and rocks,
which are usually good fish-holding places. The angler will
notice at once that the tide races are indicated by wavy lines,
and warnings that there are breaking seas in such places in
rough weather at certain states of the tide.

Now, the angler will not be fishing in rough weather, nor,
indeed, in the midst of the tide race. But experience will soon
teach him that fishing in the *neighbourhood* of such races will
provide some of the most exciting inshore fishing that can be
enjoyed around the coast of Britain. This is light boat-fishing
for that very sporting fish the tope.

19

Tackle for Tope

Tope are true sharks, and although they do not run nearly as big as blue sharks, many experienced anglers, myself included, would say that their fighting qualities are superior.

As explained in more detail later, the tope is a sporting fish rather than one for the table, but even subject to that it is perhaps in a class on its own. It can be pursued with less trouble and expense than the other members of the shark family, but will give sport that is almost as thrilling.

Tope are not lightweights. An average fish will weigh perhaps thirty pounds. The upper limit shows a fair disparity. Males may run over sixty pounds, but females may reach some ten pounds heavier. They may reach eighty pounds.

Not only is the tope a shark, but it looks like one. It has the pointed head and characteristic mouth.

They appear in our inshore waters in April, and the season runs through to October, though occasional tope are caught in the depths of winter, especially when there is a run of whiting or herring inshore. In late spring, before the mackerel arrive, they will be found concentrating on flatfish – flounders in particular – and at this time of the year are closer inshore than at any other. Later they prey on mackerel shoals, often massing

The tope belongs to the shark family.

in considerable numbers to do so. Thus, as with many of the predators, their movements are largely dependent on the migrations of the fish on which they feed.

Because the fish are big, it is assumed by too many anglers that very heavy tackle is needed to subdue them. Nothing could be farther from the truth. Tope, although powerful fighters, are *running* fish. That is to say, they do not have to be hauled by main force from the bottom, but will exhaust themselves by furious runs close to the surface – particularly in shallow water, when they will also jump excitingly.

What is needed is plenty of line, rather than strong line. Some tope experts, indeed, limit themselves to twelve pound b.s. line, and so long as they play their fish with care, there is no danger of a breakage.

The novice angler, however, would be better advised to equip himself with line around thirty pounds b.s. – at least 200 yards of it. Stiff boat-rods are not necessary – indeed they are a positive menace with light lines, since their lack of resilience may well cause a breakage. A heavy salmon-spinning rod is ideal, but a light boat-rod will do at a pinch. The reel should be a multiplier. A single-action reel is also adequate, but the danger of barked knuckles from the flying handles should always be borne in mind. The flowing trace should be of nylon-covered wire, and the hook not smaller than 6/0.

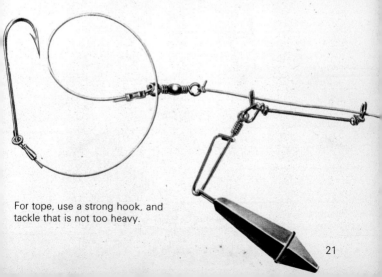

For tope, use a strong hook, and tackle that is not too heavy.

Techniques for Tope

Tope sometimes feed near the surface, but they are sought on the bottom, on clean ground. The bait must be a large one – some anglers use a whole mackerel, though it is likely that a big fillet, freshly cut, makes a better bait, since it exudes blood and oil, and will attract tope from some distance away. If fresh mackerel is not available, herring is a good substitute. Indeed, for the tope fisher in a hurry, frozen herring from the shopkeeper's deep-freeze makes a much better bait than stale herring or mackerel from the fishmonger's slab. Whiting, or even small pollack, are effective at times (though not as good as the oily species), and flounder or plaice fillets are good early in the season.

Tope fishing is almost always done with the boat at anchor. Although the odd fish will be picked up during drift-fishing, big tope in particular can be hook- and lead-shy, so that fishing to an anchor means that they need feel no resistance when they pick up the bait and run with it. (Some tope fishermen, to make sure that there is as little chance as possible of tell-tale lead resistance, pay out several fathoms of line before attaching a match-stick which stops the lead. This presents no problem on recovery, for the match-stick can be quickly broken, and the lead slides down as far as the swivel stop above the trace.)

Characteristically, a tope bite (or *run*, as it is usually called) occurs in two stages. The first is when the fish tears away with

For tope, use a large bait.

the bait, causing line to scream from the reel – the angler having from the first set the reel out of gear with the ratchet check on. Occasionally there will be a few preliminary nods at the rod-top. But to strike at this point could very likely result in a lost fish, since what is probably happening in this preliminary stage is that the tope is running with the bait just held lightly.

At the end of the first run, though, if the tope is given no cause for suspicion, there is a pause while the fish turns the bait, and a second, slower run develops. And it is at this stage that the angler must strike.

The pictures on the right illustrate this process stage by stage. When the tope is tearing away with the line – let him! But you must be ready for the moment when the first impetuous run stops, and the second, slower one begins. This is the time to strike. And you need to strike firmly.

The tope can be a very big fish, strong and wily, and can put up a powerful fight. Patience and guile, as well as a certain amount of brute strength, are needed by the angler at the beginning as well as later on when he comes to boat his catch.

The tope tears away with the bait.

Getting ready to strike.

Strike on the second run!

Boating a Tope

The angler is not left in very much doubt of the nature of what he has hold of when he gets into a tope. In deep water, it may be that much of the fighting will be done beneath the boat, but even then there will be many fast runs. In shallow water, tope will take off a hundred yards and more of line on a single run, often rolling on the surface or jumping.

This will not jeopardize the angler's tackle so long as he keeps his head and doesn't try to bring the fish to the boat's side too soon. Do not check the fish too abruptly on one of its runs. Even if the line does not break under the strain, the tope is quite likely to roll on the line – and the odds are that if it comes into contact with its sandpaper-like hide, the line will be cut through. Hurried action may result in the loss of the fish.

Holding a fine tope.

Getting ready to tail a tope.

Tope are doubtless amongst the most sporting fish that the sea angler is likely to meet, and the question must eventually arise – what is to be done with the fish once it is in the boat? Although it is said that tope is used as the basis for shark fin soup and some people insist that tope cutlets make excellent eating, the species can hardly be considered a good table fish.

However, such a large fish seems a notable prize, and the novice may want to enjoy a brief moment of glory when the boat returns to the quayside and the holiday-makers peer down at the catch.

But sooner or later killing tope seems to be useless and wasteful. The angler will want to return his fish alive to the sea, and he realizes that this is impossible if it is gaffed. Gaffing, though, is not necessary.

The 'wrist' of a tope's tail affords a good grip, and the fish can be swung aboard without any use of the gaff. The wire trace can be clipped with wire-cutters, and the tope weighed and photographed if you want, then returned to the water unharmed.

Smaller fish can be set free without their even being taken from the sea, if the boat has not too much freeboard. Don't try to remove the hook : any attempt to do so will almost certainly kill the fish. Tope seem to 'digest' an undisturbed hook.

Inshore Bay Fishing

Around the British Isles, intensive trawling has meant that resident species, on easily accessible, clean ground inshore, have been greatly thinned out. This is particularly true along the southern and eastern coasts of the country.

However, despite this, there are excellent opportunities for the angler with rod and line. These arise from the seasonal migration of fish of some species. Notable examples are the autumn and winter run of whiting and cod along the shores of the English Channel and the East Coast.

Much of this fishing is in areas that are close inshore, and small boats that would be quite out of place on an Atlantic coast can be used to get amongst the fish.

This inshore bay fishing, to use a convenient phrase, is short-range work, and takes place on comparatively shallow ground at five to fifteen fathoms. This ground is usually clean, and is sand, or sand with rough patches. Scattered areas of small, weedy stones of the kind commonly found on such ground are valuable gathering points for fish, and local knowledge of the whereabouts of such patches can be of the greatest angling value.

This is dinghy fishing, fourteen- and sixteen-footers with outboard motors being ideal for the job, though it must be confessed that their use is somewhat limited by the force of the wind. Against this can be set the advantage that they can be towed by a car and launched straight off the beach.

In this case, as always in using small open boats, stringent precautions must be taken. In dinghy fishing or when using dinghies for any other purpose, there is not the freedom to stand up at will.

A dinghy is not very large, and can be very much affected by the elements, without the added hazards of forgetful or unwise movements in the boat.

It is affected by even slight roughness of the water, and 'keeping the weight low' by remaining seated is the safest rule to follow, especially for beginners.

Another practical point arises from the smallness of a dinghy. Anglers working in rather cramped conditions have to work as a team. Only in this way can fouling of lines and tackle be kept to a minimum.

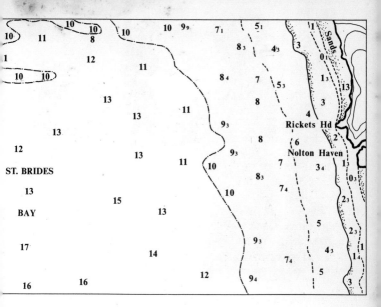

How depths are shown on a chart. The large numerals show
fathoms; under eleven fathoms, both fathoms and feet are given.

A fourteen-foot dinghy.

A nice cod and (right) a codling.

Cod, Whiting and Dabs

The first fish to arrive inshore in the autumn are the whiting. Small whiting are present right through the year and can be bait-robbing nuisances when they take what is meant for better fish. But the autumn run of whiting from deeper water – often called 'Channel whiting' – are different. To begin with, they are much bigger, averaging more than a pound apiece. Some of the large fish reach two or three pounds. And they are present in great numbers at times. It would be idle to pretend that they offer sport of high quality – they are rather too numerous and too easy to catch for that, as well as not being large enough to endanger even the lightest tackle. But a crisp autumn morning afloat, with the whiting shoals biting merrily, has much to recommend it, especially as a change after a dour spell in pursuit of a more demanding species.

When the cod follow, as they do later in the autumn, then of course much bigger fish are available. A remarkable feature of the British sea-angling scene in the last few years has been the enormous increase in the quantity and quality of the cod

The dab is a small flatfish.

which have approached our inshore waters late in the year. These fish run to a considerable size – a cod taken on rod and line in 1965 off Barry, Glamorganshire, weighed forty-four pounds.

The area in which this record fish was taken is, curiously enough, somewhat remote from those which have been the most productive in terms of numbers of fish. The eastern corner of England from, roughly, Great Yarmouth round to Rye Bay, has provided the best sport of all. Fish weighing twenty pounds and more have been commonplace, and a thirty-pounder, at the very least, is needed before eye-brows are raised in such places as Deal or Felixstowe.

Delicious little dabs turn up each winter at roughly the same time as the cod, and fulfil a useful function by taking freely at times when other fish are reluctant to feed. This is perhaps rather more marked in shore fishing than it is from boats.

Top right are shown the cod on their way down the coast in the autumn migration. Whiting move eastwards towards Kent. So the south-east and east coasts become at times favourite areas for both species. Some codling appear early in the year.

Codling ▲ Cod ■
Dab ● Whiting ☐

29

Inshore Tackle and Baits

For inshore bay fishing, tackle need be neither elaborate nor expensive. Any single-action reel will do so long as it is resistant to salt-water corrosion and is of sufficient diameter (around five inches) to permit a quick retrieve. Perfection in this field, though, is represented by a two-speed multiplying reel like the Abu 9000, which retrieves at a very high gear ratio when the angler is coming up simply to re-bait, but which automatically changes to a low ratio when there is considerable resistance – as when a fish is on the hook.

A medium-action, hollow-glass boat-rod is useful. Small fish such as whiting will not make very much impression on it, but it makes for more sporting fishing with cod of six pounds and upwards, and is capable of subduing some very big fish indeed.

The line – monofilament or braided synthetic – need not be heavier than twenty pounds b.s., though the majority of anglers use line that is nearer the thirty-five pound mark or even stouter. The drawback of heavy line is that it needs heavy weights

Rod and reel for inshore bay fishing.

to counteract the greater tide resistance, and heavy weights diminish sport and pleasure.

The end tackle should be a simple two- or three-hook paternoster. The size of hook used will depend on the size of the bait and the class of fish you are expecting – a No. 6/0 at one extreme for big cod, and a long-shanked No. 6 for dabs.

Bait will vary enormously, but lugworm remains a solid favourite. Remember, though, that a big cod needs a large mouthful. Many anglers, on the South Coast particularly, are dependent upon shop-bought lugworms, and these tend to be small creatures: I have crammed a dozen or more on to a single big hook when I have been expecting big Channel cod. A single small lugworm, on the other hand, will be perfectly adequate for dabs and whiting.

Fish baits – usually sprat or herring cut into strips – are also effective in winter fishing for cod and whiting, especially when there is a considerable inshore movement of sprats. Less usual baits – clam, razor fish, mussel and squid, for example – are just as effective as the standard ones. Thus the latitude in regard to baits for fishing of this type is considerable.

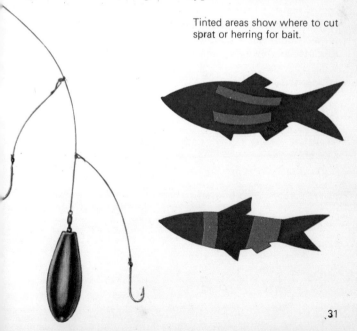

Tinted areas show where to cut sprat or herring for bait.

ESTUARY FISHING

Estuary fishing is an art in its own right, and involves different techniques from those that apply in the open sea, and from those of open coast. And estuaries themselves vary enormously, from quite small creeks to broad expanses of water for which a boat really is needed.

But they have this in common: so long as there is no serious pollution, they will hold fish in plenty. It doesn't need much thought to decide why this is so. The estuary is a nursery for small fish, from herring fry to tiny flounders no bigger than a postage stamp. The lack of a violent surf means that creatures of the marine littoral – worms and shellfish in particular – are numerous. Fast tides are to be expected in the estuary, which often cuts new banks in mud or sand and reveals marine animals. There is also the possibility of food being swept down from the river above, though this is not as important as the other factors mentioned.

Thus, an estuary becomes a happy hunting-ground for a number of important species. At the mouth of a large estuary, tope are to be found preying on the flounders which move up and down the channels. Bass and mullet will venture much farther than the tope, right into brackish water, where there is a kind of no-man's-land, for brown trout from the river above will also establish themselves in the same zone. (They are then

A sand estuary.

High water at Dover.

Six hours after high water at Dover.

Tides in Britain, shown in close detail in tide-tables and on charts, can be presented in general terms by diagrams like these. Such diagrams may show the tidal position at, say, hourly intervals before and after high water at Dover.

called 'slob trout'.) Flounders, quite large ones sometimes, will be found almost everywhere, and on high tides pelagic species like mackerel and garfish will venture a little way in.

There is enormous variety from the angling point of view, but for the moment we can look at some of the more specialized aspects of estuary fishing – the techniques that apply to the capture of mullet, bass, flounders and shad, for instance, in such surroundings.

One of the most important focal points is the bar of a sand estuary, where the tide builds up for some time before breaking through to the estuary proper. Then there are tidal pools, where fish are held up, or choose to pause on their way upstream. Near the bar, and in the tidal pools, are the points where the maximum fishing effort should be made.

Knowing this, you can assess the possibilities of the area and avoid quite unpromising spots in favour of those in which you have a better chance of obtaining good sport.

General Estuary Fishing

Specialized fishing requires specialist tackle, which will be described later. But estuaries, inevitably, have a great attraction for the holiday angler, who is often without specialized gear and simply wants an hour or two of fishing. For him, an ordinary beach-casting outfit will produce fish, though not so many as he could expect with more serious fishing.

The outfit might consist of a ten- or eleven-foot glass rod, and one of the big sea-sized fixed spool reels, loaded with twenty-pound b.s. monofilament nylon. A paternoster

Tackle for general estuary fishing.

end tackle (tied direct on the line with blood-loops) is adequate for this purpose, and the hook should be in the range No. 1 to No. 2/0, covering school bass and flounder.

The baits that are actually to be obtained in the estuary will catch fish best. These are ragworm, lug, mussel, clam and crab.

The mention of this last bait recalls one of the chief hazards of this kind of fishing. Estuaries are the homes of millions of crabs, and in some spots your hooks may be stripped clean very quickly. Oddly enough, crabs themselves (used in the soft or peeler stages) are often more proof against the attentions of their relatives than are the other baits. Constant checking of the bait when you are bottom-fishing an estuary prevents the bait being lost without your knowing about it.

This can actually happen – and you would feel rather frustrated if you discovered that you had apparently been angling for some time after your bait had vanished without your knowledge!

The rod, meanwhile, should be hand-held, for bass, moving up the estuary at speed, hit a bait hard once, and give no second chance. Only flounders, of all the species that are likely to be found, will swallow the bait and hook themselves.

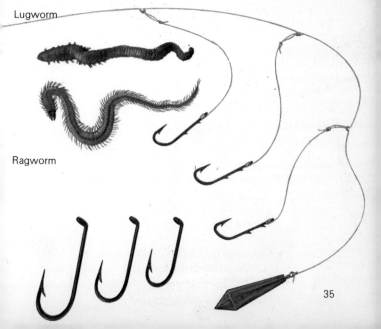

Lugworm

Ragworm

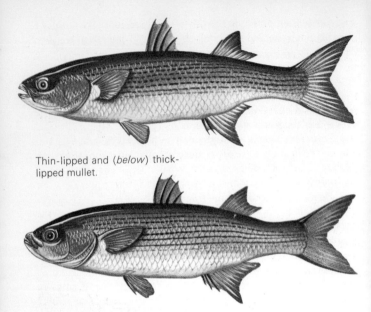

Thin-lipped and (*below*) thick-lipped mullet.

The Exasperating Mullet

Mullet are the most exasperating fish in the sea. No marine species shows itself more often. On a summer's evening, the estuary is full of the typical V-patterns, as mullet slowly cruise upstream, just bulging the surface film. No fish would seem to be easier prey, but in fact, the estuary mullet presents about the most difficult angling problem that exists in salt water.

A close look at a mullet's mouth gives a clue to the difficulty. Here is no predatory fish that will give chase to a bright lure! Indeed, it looks as if the mullet is equipped for browsing, not biting, and this is in fact the case. The whole problem of mullet fishing stems from the diet of the species, which in natural circumstances is based on tiny sea-creatures and plants.

Its usual diet is food of this kind. So many methods of fishing that have proved their value with more voracious fish are 'out' as far as mullet are concerned.

Three grey mullet species occur in British waters. The golden grey mullet is such a rarity that it need not concern us here. The second is the thin-lipped species, the third the thick-lipped. This last-named is by far the most common in

Atlantic waters as far north as Britain. It seems that in Ireland, only this species occurs. The thin-lipped species occurs in quite large numbers off the coast of Devon and Cornwall. In the Mediterranean this is the species that predominates.

The thin-lipped grey mullet seems to be less hook-shy than the thick-lipped, is more a fish of the open coast, and presents fewer difficulties in the capture – as, possibly, is indicated by very large catches of mullet occasionally reported from the West Country, running into more than a hundred fish at a session by a couple of rods. Meanwhile, the odds are that most estuary fish are thick-lipped, making them as difficult a proposition as there is in salt water.

However, the sea angler should not allow himself to be unduly daunted by the difficulties. They only increase the thrill of the chase, and if it is successful they make the capture the more worth while; so in the next section we shall go more deeply into ways and means of catching these tantalizingly elusive fish.

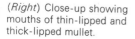
(*Right*) Close-up showing mouths of thin-lipped and thick-lipped mullet.

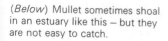
(*Below*) Mullet sometimes shoal in an estuary like this – but they are not easy to catch.

Ragworm

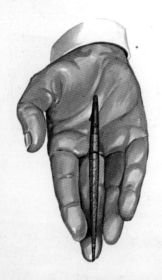

Freshwater floats can be used for mullet.

For years, a controversy has raged amongst sea fishermen as to whether mullet are *really* a shy and cautious species or whether they are, in fact, simply giving the impression of shyness because they are not interested in the angler's bait. Fresh point is given to the argument on occasions when mullet seem to go quite wild, taking almost any bait, even if presented on the crudest tackle. There may be a good reason for this, as we shall see in a moment, but meanwhile, the paradoxical nature of the species is underlined.

The fascination of mullet is that their behaviour is anything but predictable. Sometimes they take readily, at others, they are shy and elusive. They may swim near the surface or disappear, perhaps into deeper water with, it seems, the speed of lightning.

Light Gear

Whatever the truth is, there seems to be no point at all in using heavy gear in normal mullet fishing. Specialist mullet tackle, in fact, is about the lightest used in sea fishing: the estuarial surroundings make this possible.

The best rod for mullet is the freshwater kind that is

used for such species as tench and small carp. It is usually known as the Avon type. This is lively enough to cast the light float tackle normally used and is strong enough to subdue a lively fish like the mullet that runs normally to five or six pounds but which may attain much larger weights, even double figures, possibly. This rod is used in conjunction with a small fixed-spool reel loaded with six-pound b.s. line. Fresh-water floats are needed, some split shot and a supply of eyed No. 6 hooks.

Cheesepaste also appeals to mullet.

There are more baits listed in the sea-fishing textbooks for mullet than for any other salt-water species. Banana cubes, macaroni, bacon fat . . . the exotic list is endless. This, however, is not because mullet will eat practically anything. It is a sign of ex-asperated experimenting!

However, there is no need to worry about this huge variety. A close look at the list will show that nearly all the baits mentioned are (a) soft, and (b) white. Cheesepaste or breadpaste will do instead of any of these, and the only other important mullet-bait is tiny harbour ragworm.

Both 'fancy' and plain baits are effective.

A centre-pin reel, made as light as possible for free running.

39

Catching the Elusive Mullet

For successful mullet fishing, the first requirement is the liberal use of ground bait in an estuary pool where the fish stay to feed. Finding a pool of this kind is not easy, but you must shrewdly assess the local waters. Travelling mullet are a well-nigh impossible proposition for the angler; but when the fish linger and cruise around in a pool, often at low tide, then there is decidedly a chance of catching them.

Once a shoal of mullet has been located, an intensive baiting-up programme must be started. The object of this is to wean the fish from their regular diet to items of food that can be presented on a hook when the time comes.

The ground bait can consist of bread-and-bran mixture with pilchard oil and small ragworms added. In some areas, a mashed-up paste of shrimp is used. But the main thing to be remembered is that samples of the hook bait should be included.

It may be several days before this policy begins to work, but eventually it will do so, and then sport can be fast and furious.

Baiting up with harbour ragworm.

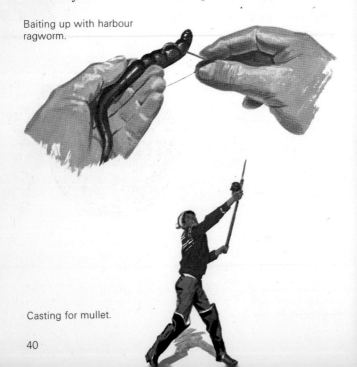

Casting for mullet.

A landing net should always be used for mullet.

Even when mullet are taking well, however, it still pays to be cautious, and it is worth while to remember that early morning and late evening fishing give the best results, where these times coincide with the vital tide times.

Besides ground-baiting and choosing your time, there is still a very definite technique for catching these fish.

When you hook mullet the float will often sink boldly, but no contact is made on the strike! Only experience will teach you how to get the timing right, but it should be said that more fish are hooked if it is possible to fish under the rod-top and strike by lifting the rod-tip.

Mullet play very hard, and should not be 'horsed', since their mouths are, in part, soft, and tear easily. A landing net is essential for these fish.

Gulls may circle over the water where bass are shoaling.

School Bass

Like mullet, bass that run the estuary betray their presence by movement on the surface. But there is no possibility of confusing the two species, even when the fish themselves cannot be seen. Bass move more quickly, and, instead of V-ripples, make splashy, purposeful swirls at the surface. Generally speaking, they move through in small groups, and often it is not possible to take more than a brace of fish from each group before they disappear up- or downstream.

Also, unlike the mullet, these bass are feeding on small fish, either brit (the fry of herrings and sprats) or sand eels (the latter only in sandy estuaries). They can be caught, and give excellent sport, on light tackle.

We are currently trying to persuade anglers to return as many bass as possible alive to the water, as they are somewhat threatened by commercial fishing.

Such bass are nearly always the kind sea fishermen call

'schoolies', running from one pound or so in weight to roughly four pounds. Much bigger specimens will find their way into the estuary from time to time, but the greater part of the fishing is with school bass.

These moving fish are best sought in the fastest tide runs of the estuary, though they may be picked up in other places too. In a long estuary, it is best for the angler to keep moving. For instance, the first hour of the tide is almost always good right at the estuary mouth, but after that it is best to move higher up to another vantage point. In practice, this often means taking to the car and driving upstream to meet the fish again. The converse holds good on the ebb tide, with the proviso that the fish often drop back at the first sign of falling water and cover the ground much more quickly than they do on the flow. So catching estuary bass is largely a matter of knowing where they are and what they are going to do at different states of the tide.

In a big estuary, however, where large, deep pools form, some bass may remain right through the tide, and such places are useful standbys when one has lost contact with the big shoals. It should be possible to identify likely pools.

The main channel of the estuary is easier to reach at low tide.

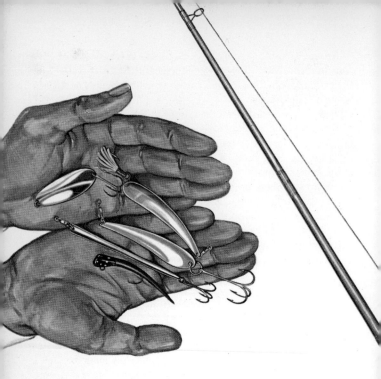

Rod and reel for spinning for bass, and lures of various shapes and colours.

Spinning for School Bass

There is not a little thrill and excitement to be gained from pitting your wits against the school bass in this way – presenting him with your lure, and waiting in suspense to see whether it will attract him.

Moreover, spinning of this kind has an advantage in that really light tackle can be used. I recommend nothing heavier than a glass trout-spinning rod, and a small fixed-spool reel loaded with five-pound b.s. line, which will enable comparatively small baits to be cast. The only exception to this is where weedy rocks along the shoreline put such light tackle in hazard when it comes to landing a fish. In such a case, the remedy is for the tackle to be scaled up.

In this kind of fishing, it is often possible to 'fish the rise' so to speak, and cast to individual fish that can be seen breaking the surface. You will gain a general idea of the direction of movement of the shoal, and the best idea is to cast ahead of them so that the lure will swing 'across their bows'.

School bass respond best to a lure which is fished as fast as possible. They have been taken when the bait was skating over the surface rather than working below it. In this respect bass react in the same way as sea trout in a marine context.

Although a normal fixed-spool reel has been specified as adequate, the angler will find himself at a decided advantage if he has one of the special fast retrieve models that are now available.

Successful lures are long, narrow, slightly dished spoons, Devon minnows and wagtails. The basic colour should be silver, and the size used is dependent on the kind of bait-fish that the bass are taking. The range is quite a wide one between five inches and one inch, and the successful angler is the one who experiments until he has found an acceptable size.

45

Flounders are nearly always present in estuaries, but from the New Year to March they spawn out at sea.

Baited Spoon for Flounders

Flounders are hardly exciting fish when they take the bottom-fished bait of an angler who is using heavy gear! But in an estuary, if light tackle is used, they can provide a certain amount of sport – sport that is more valuable in the absence of better fish; for unlike bass and mullet, flounders can be relied upon to be present almost always, except for a short period between the New Year and March, when they move out to sea to spawn.

Plaice and dabs are liable to be confused with the flounder: perhaps because they are all flatfish. However, plaice and dabs are not often taken right inside estuaries. The orange spots that sometimes appear on the dark side (which is brownish green) are not as vivid as those on plaice, and they fade quite quickly after death. If a problem of identification should arise, the surest test is to run a finger along the plainly-marked lateral line of the fish. A hard ridge of spiny scales will give an impression of roughness if the fish is indeed a flounder.

Flounders will take a bottom-fished bait in the estuary – lugworm, ragworm and soft crab are all good – but the most interesting way is by means of the baited spoon. This is worked best by trailing it behind a slowly-moving boat, but at a pinch it can be cast from the shore. The bait is usually a small lugworm, and it should be noted that the bait itself does not spin, but only the spoon.

Flounders, in spite of their appearance, have a strong predatory instinct. They will come right up off the bottom to take the moving bait. The lighter the tackle you are able to use, the greater the sport will be.

If you are definitely going after flounders, forget their playful habit of nipping off bait meant for more exciting fish, and choose your tackle accordingly.

All in all the flounder, even if it can hardly be regarded as a top-flight sporting fish, will nevertheless provide amusing fishing in places and at times when other fish are not available.

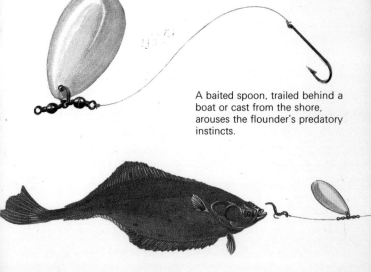

A baited spoon, trailed behind a boat or cast from the shore, arouses the flounder's predatory instincts.

The Sporting Shad

Shad, like salmon and sea-trout, are anadromous fish. In other words, they do the greater part of their feeding at sea, and enter fresh water for the purpose of spawning. Shad, therefore, come within the orbit both of fresh- and salt-water anglers, and are most likely to be encountered by the latter in estuary fishing.

There are two species in British Waters – the Allis Shad and the Twaite Shad. They are not unlike the herring in appearance. Both species when they are young have a row of black spots – one behind the gills, and the others running back at intervals along the top of the fish's side. In the Allis Shad the spots have gone by the time the fish is fully grown.

Shad are most common in our southern and south-western estuaries, notably those of the Severn and Wye, and are present for only a short season, about six weeks from mid-May to mid-June. They are rather too bony to make good table fish.

But both species – the Allis and the Twaite shad – make up for this by their sporting qualities. Although neither is a particularly large fish –

(*Above*) Lures for shad. (*Below*) Using a lure for shad in a Severn weirpool. Shad are anadromous fish: they can live both in fresh and in salt water.

about a pound and a half being an average weight – they can be successfully taken on very light spinning tackle, and these 'Mayfish', as they are called on the Wye, are as game and as lively as the freshest of sea trout.

A trout spinning outfit is the heaviest that should be used, and the line can be as light as two pounds b.s. Indeed, it has to be as light as possible so that the very small lures that make the best shad baits can be cast.

Fly spoons are ideal, and the smallest size of Mepps bar spoon is about the best killer of shad that I know. When the run is on, the fish can be picked up almost anywhere; but the higher up the estuary, the easier it is to pinpoint the fish.

Shad take the lure freely, though they have very hard mouths, which results very often in their being merely pricked, not hooked. Make sure that hooks are needle-sharp, and handle the fish lightly.

These are the main points in fishing for shad – not a great prize for the table, but a species that can provide a good day's sport in the right places and at the right time of year.

ATLANTIC STORM BEACHES

The wide Atlantic beaches of the western and south-western coastlines of Britain provide fishing that is possibly more attractive than any other in sea angling.

The main quarry on such beaches is bass. Other species – flounders, gurnards, even dogfish – are taken from time to time, but it is bass the surf fisherman has come for – the silver and big-shouldered bass of the Atlantic surf, that will swim to the shore, almost, into a foot or so of creamy water when chasing after its prey.

Why do bass visit Atlantic storm beaches? At first sight, such places seem barren of food. Not even a lugworm finds shelter on many of them, so constant is the surf. But when a five-day storm has pounded the beach with huge seas, many small marine creatures are washed into the surf from farther out, and shoals of sand eels may find themselves close in.

The ideal time to fish is when the sea is settling after such a storm. During the storm, the seas make it impossible to keep

A typical storm beach.

Atlantic storm beach — the best position after a storm.
Left: Too rough. *Right:* Too calm. *Centre:* Conditions suitable.

the bait in the water, and even the muscular bass may be reluctant to venture inshore. A falling sea, however, has an irresistible attraction for bass, and the third or fourth tide after the wind has stopped blowing is the time to go fishing.

Then the breakers will have settled into sets of three and four, with long tables of foamy water between them. The bass seem to feed for the most part behind the second or third breakers, but sometimes they will venture so close in that the angler, wading out to cast, will disturb them in the shallows.

The surf angler therefore must know in which direction each of his local beaches faces, so that he can judge which of them is 'coming into form' according to the direction of the wind and of the seas breaking on the beach.

The picture on this page shows for the sake of clarity an example where the differences between beaches are more noticeably marked than usual.

Where the food is: bass feeding behind breakers.

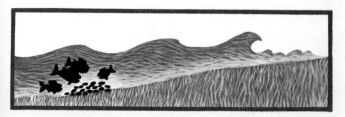

Surf-casting Tackle and Bait

The strength of the surf, and the necessity of casting the bait a hundred yards or more out to sea, means that somewhat specialized tackle is required. This should be chosen with care because of the special conditions encountered in fishing from beaches in heavy surf.

The rod is of hollow fibreglass, between eleven feet and thirteen feet long (depending on the physique of the caster) and double tapered – that is, the fibreglass, which extends into the handle of the rod, narrows in diameter towards the butt, giving a bow-like action. The reel is a narrow-spooled multiplier, mounted high on the butt so that a double-handed grip can be taken. The line is monofilament, between fifteen pounds and twenty pounds b.s., but the last twenty feet is of thirty pounds b.s., to provide a 'collar' to take the shock load of casting the lead.

The end tackle is a simple paternoster, made with two blood-loops to take the hooks (2/0 and 3/0 are useful sizes) and ending in a link swivel to which the lead is attached.

The size of the lead will depend on the force of the surf; but

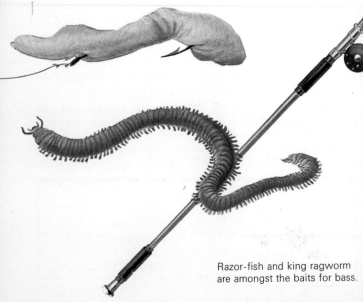

Razor-fish and king ragworm are amongst the baits for bass.

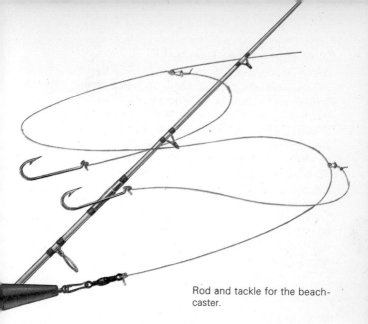
Rod and tackle for the beach-caster.

so long as wire grips are used, there is rarely any need for it to be heavier than four ounces.

The angler himself should wear thigh boots, or better still latex chest waders. In the latter case, care should be taken, as wading out too far could put the angler in serious danger when there is a heavy sea running.

A variety of baits will take bass in these conditions. The most common is lugworm, which, however, is often more effective at night than in the daytime, possibly because of its strong smell. On account of its liveliness, king ragworm is a more effective daylight bait. Shellfish are good, too – especially substantial shellfish like the clam and the razor fish. These have the added advantage of being tough baits, and stay well on the hook during a powerful cast. Squid strips, even small squids used whole, are first-class, especially as a night bait, and there are times when soft or peeler crab is effective. Fish-baits like mackerel, herring strip and kipper are favoured by some anglers. Large bass seem to have a predilection for 'high' baits. Various other baits have been used. But there is no standard bait, and only the favourites are given above. This still leaves plenty of room for experiment!

Surf-casting Techniques

In the last decade, considerable advances have been made in rod and reel design, and it has naturally followed that new techniques of casting have developed to take advantage of this. Surf-casting in particular has developed into a specialized business, and bearing in mind that the angler who can cast a long way into the breakers is often (although not always) the man who catches the most fish, then it is important that the sea angler should adopt the best technique possible, so that he can use his rod and the power of his muscles to the greatest advantage.

The method illustrated here is the 'lay-back' style, developed by Leslie Moncrieff. The tackle is a double-tapered rod of hollow fibreglass, as already described, and a narrow-spooled multiplying reel.

Swinging the bait back, then far, far out into the surf.

Moncrieff emphasizes the fact that if the right techniques are used very little muscle power is needed to throw the bait 130–150 yards. Style and co-ordination are everything.

You can see from the picture how the actions are carried out – or perhaps it would be better to say are developed. Note that at the start the rod is carried right back. This is to get it into the right position for the first stage in casting. Next it is brought across the front of the body, and as this movement develops the rod is bowed with the force and speed imparted to it. Finally the bait is thrown out into the water. This technique, incidentally, can be demonstrated, and practised up to a point, on dry land as well as on the beach.

The whole idea is to achieve distance and accuracy of placing, and a systematic method is necessary for this.

Keenly alert, the beach angler fishes the surf.

Bass: Stance and Bite Detection

Having made the cast, and sent the bait anything between 50 and 150 yards out, the angler has a waiting game to play.

First he has taken up the slack line until he feels the resistance of the lead – firm if he is using wire grips as an auxiliary, not so fixed if there are no attachments to the lead to hold it in the sand. Where possible he dispenses with grips, for apart from the inconvenience of pulling them through the sand on the retrieve, they do not permit any movement of the bait, or very little. They are necessary when the surf is heavy, or when there is a strong lateral pull on the tide – but only then.

The angler who is fishing a lead that rolls a little with the tide has to keep on the alert all the time. He must learn to distinguish between the bumps and taps caused by the lead's movement and the take of a fish. Judging a bass bite is not always easy. Small fish will rattle merrily at the bait, and big ones sometimes pull the rod-top down very purposefully, but often really big specimens very lightly tap the bait. To strike or not to strike. The answer here must be that one should strike at the least suspicion of a knock.

Another type of take which deceives the novice is the slack-line bait. Here the lead's resistance suddenly disappears – the fish in fact has picked up the bait and is moving the lead inshore. This is not to be confused with a steady slackening of the line when an extra-big wave lifts the lead. The slack-line bite proper is quite dramatic, and an instant response must be made.

Where and how the angler takes up his stance is important. The best place for him is in the water, as far as he can risk going without getting wet (PVC trousers worn over waders help a lot). This means that he is as near as possible to a taking fish; and the nearer he is, the more positive the strike can be.

But hooking the fish is only part of what can be quite a complicated procedure, so it pays to have an understanding of the ways of your quarry.

Grips for heavy surf or a strong lateral tide.

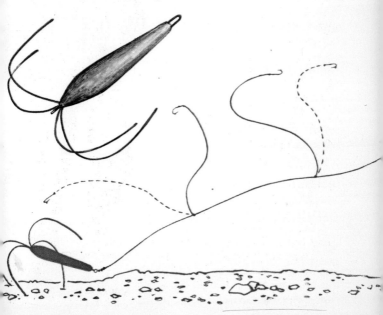

Playing the Bass

Once you have hooked it, you can judge the size of a bass in the surf fairly easily.

You will find that fish under four pounds put up a steady resistance, but you can keep them on the move without a great deal of trouble. Bigger bass give an impression of great solidity, and there are usually two stages in the fight.

It is just as well to itemize these, so that you can be prepared for them when they occur, and be ready to take the appropriate action.

Early on come the runs, sometimes out to sea, very often straight in towards the angler. The second tactic is the more dangerous, for there is always the chance of the fish being allowed a slack line, so that if he is only slightly hooked, the hook may simply fall out of his mouth. The angler's counter-move in this event is to run backwards up the sand as quickly as possible, until contact is made.

This will keep the line taut, and will make sure that when you feel your fish again he will really have taken the hook, and will be unable to shed it and make his escape.

The second stage in the fish's fight occurs when the bass has been brought into shallow water, often when his back breaks the surface.

Remember that the fish will sometimes turn wild at this stage, splashing furiously and putting up a fierce resistance to the pressure of the line!

This may be all very well from the sporting point of view, but remember that you must keep control of the proceedings, or you may lose your fish. In fact, it is a highly dangerous stage in the fight, and too determined an effort to 'horse' the fish ashore can result in a broken trace, especially if the fish is a big one. The best plan is to keep up a steady pressure and walk back slowly, taking care to stop the moment the resistance increases to the critical mark – something that is easy to judge with a little experience. The waves themselves can be a help: try to time your effort so that it coincides with a wave which is running up the beach.

Most bass can be gradually run aground in this way, and the angler can secure his fish by slipping his hand under the gill-cover and lifting it from the water. (Bass are armed with a spike on the gill-case, so take care!) If the fish is a very big one, or if you are a little nervous, then a small, very sharp gaff can be used. Gaff under the gill-case, not in the side, for the tough scales of a bass will very often repel the point. Don't gaff or run your bass aground until it is well beaten and is at least partly out of the water. Landing nets are a possibility on steep-to beaches but, generally speaking, they are more trouble than they are worth when you are landing a bass.

Beaching the bass: having run his fish aground, the angler, his line still taut, prepares to gaff the bass under the gill-case.

STEEP SHINGLE BEACHES

If the long, sandy beach, pounded by Atlantic rollers, is typical of the western shores of these islands, the shingle beach, steep-to and with a significant depth of water a very short distance offshore, is characteristic of the Channel coast and of the littoral farther north.

Such beaches, because of their configuration, require quite different techniques and tackle from those of the West. In addition, the species which haunt them are different: cod, dabs and sole replace bass and flounders. (No hard-and-fast rule can be laid down. Bass will come on to shingle beaches sometimes, and cod will turn up in the western surf: but not typically.)

The chief problem of the shingle beach is that the shingle itself is barren. The sandworms, crustaceans and molluscs that live in sand are completely absent, so why should fish approach shingle beaches at all?

One might reasonably ask what there is in the way of food to attract them. This problem is perhaps not easy to solve at once, but it is cleared up when the beach is uncovered at

Careful placing of the bait is the secret of steep shingle-beach fishing.

low spring tides. It will then be seen that the shingle bank gives way to flat, hard sand towards the limit of the tides. This sand holds quantities of food, which is often washed out by wave action, especially, of course, in big seas. The steep shingle bank and the flat sand meet at an angle – a kind of natural gutter where food accumulates and fish feed.

Hence the important thing to remember when you are fishing a shingle beach is to aim to throw the bait as nearly as possible into this gutter.

This is the area in which food is to be found, and where the fish expect to find it. So it is also the area in which the bait must be placed. A bait landing on the shingle itself will not be found: the fish will not hunt beyond the sand line. A bait thrown out on to the clean sand *may* be taken, but the chances are greater if the bait is snugly in the gutter.

At Dungeness, which may be regarded as a classic example of the Channel shingle beach, a tidal eddy at the Point forms what local anglers know as 'the Dustbin'. It is a kind of natural dumping ground for small marine animals.

On shingle beaches, long-distance casting techniques are vital for success in placing the bait.

Where sand and shingle meet, there is a 'natural gutter' that collects food and attracts fish.

Shingle Beaches: Tackle and Bait

The beach-casting tackle suitable for such beaches as Dungeness is determined by two factors: the considerable distance that has to be cast, and the fairly substantial lead (six to eight ounces) that has to be used to hold the baits out at the feeding grounds. Strong currents parallel to the shore demand this.

The rod is therefore much more powerful than the one used for bass on western beaches, though it shares the same principles of design – double tapered, of hollow glass, and with a long grip for casting, the grip being occasionally as long as thirty-six inches. The reel is a narrow-spooled multiplier for distance casting, and it is loaded with thirty-pound line and an even heavier 'collar' – a length of line to take the shockload of the cast and to beach a fish. (It is important that the collar be long enough to be wound a few turns on the reel.)

The end tackle is a paternoster, with two or three hooks. Some anglers use simple blood-loops to take the hooks; others reinforce them with plastic tubes (often, conveniently, the empty

Beach casting requires a powerful rod.

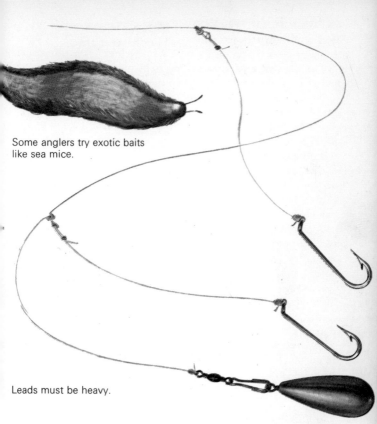

Some anglers try exotic baits like sea mice.

Leads must be heavy.

tubes of ball-point pens). The lead (almost invariably one with wire grips to hold it in position) is attached to the end of the paternoster by means of a link swivel. The hooks, looped on, will be 4/0, unless the angler wishes to try for dabs at the same time, when one of his hooks will be a long-shanked No. 6.

Baits are, commonly, lugworm and herring. Where big cod are concerned, a really big bait is much more attractive than a small one. Some anglers have had considerable success on shingle beaches by experimenting with unusual ones – including sea mice and razor fish.

There is no objection to trying out new ideas, at least to the extent of seeing whether the new bait attracts.

Shingle Beaches: Winter Cod

Cod more than other fish are the quarry of most shingle-beach anglers. So popular are the Kentish beaches within reach of London that an early start has to be made to ensure a good position on the beach, and even then many anglers will have arrived in the dark hours, not to mention those who fish right through the night.

For large numbers of anglers the area is a favourite not only because it is within easy reach but also for reasons connected with the seasonal movements of cod.

The best months for this fishing are from October to January, though in good years the season will be extended. (This refers to big cod, up to thirty pounds or so. Small codling can be taken almost throughout the year.)

A combination of two factors brings the big cod into places like Dungeness. Spawning is the first of them, an inshore migration taking place each autumn. The stocks of fish come from the North Sea and far out in the Channel, and the past five years have seen them come inshore in enormous numbers although, as we have seen, the necessity for very long casts means that the most skilful and best-equipped anglers take a disproportionate share of the catches.

The second factor is the movement of sprat shoals, which is important. The sprats tend to move about a great deal, and many of the cod follow them, so that an offshore movement of the bait fish can mean poor sport. Cod, of course, will take bait of many kinds besides sprats. Herring also (cut in strips for angling) is well liked, but the cod is not too choosey. Other baits include razor fish, lugworm, etc.

The best conditions occur after a gale, when the sandy bottom has been torn up, and thousands of small creatures are swept inshore. The effect of a gale can be clearly seen at Dungeness, where astute locals beachcomb the tide-line, picking up lugworms and shellfish in quantity, and selling them to anglers from the city, who are quite unaware that the harvest is there and free for all!

Cod are not such tearaway feeders as bass, and the rod can be safely propped in a rest, the angler waiting until the jerking of the rod-tip indicates a well-hooked fish. The heavy tackle used makes landing all but the biggest cod an easy matter. The only dangerous moment comes when a fish is brought on to the shingle: then the undertow can put an enormous strain on the tackle. Using the wave action to beach the fish is the best method, and a gaff is a great help as well.

The picture below shows a cod brought to a shingle beach by the use of the gaff. The main consideration is to get the cod away from the water while saving the tackle from unnecessary strain.

Spawning grounds (dark blue) of the cod. Generally speaking, big cod go to the main spawning area in January, but around the coasts of Kent they are taken from October up to about the end of March.

A cod beached in shingle.

Shingle Beaches: Autumn Soles

A fish of Channel beaches that is attracting more and more attention from specialist anglers is the sole. This fish is more likely to be taken in calm conditions than in rough, and at night rather than in the daytime. (If it is caught by day, it may be because the water is dark in colour.) Soles are much more common on British beaches than they are ever thought to be by the average angler. The reason is one that may not be realized by the inexperienced, and it is quite simple. They are not taken because the tackle used will not hook them: even a big sole, of two pounds or more, has a tiny mouth, and since hooks of Size 8 and below are not commonly used, soles are not often beached.

Another point to remember about soles is that they rarely move far beyond the low-tide mark. This means that fishing is virtually limited to an hour or so on either side of low water, and after that stage another species had better be sought. Night fishing, around low water, in clear conditions, is the best.

Use small hooks for the sole's tiny mouth.

These practical points about the sole's physical characteristics and its feeding habits show clearly the importance of learning as much as you can about your quarry. This will not only increase your chances of success – and often avoid tiresome discouragement – but will make your sport very much more interesting.

It cannot be pretended that soles are a sporting species. They are much too small for that, and in any case the tackle which has to be used to cast the bait out precludes it. But of course they are a great prize, like turbot, and the angler who takes home half a dozen big soles needs no excuse for several months at least to go out fishing!

A three-hook paternoster tackle is generally used, though in calm conditions there is no reason why a running ledger should not be employed. Soles are fish that cannot be given too much time to take the bait. They will hook themselves, and the angler has no problem here. The actual food of the sole is varied, and what one would expect to find in its preferred surroundings. It includes mussels, hermit, crab, shrimp, various worms, and a variety of other marine creatures. The bait to use is lugworm. Shop-bought lugworms are often too small to be of much use for species like cod, but they are ideal for soles. A very good bait, if you can get hold of it, is the white ragworm, found in clean sand, often in lugworm beds.

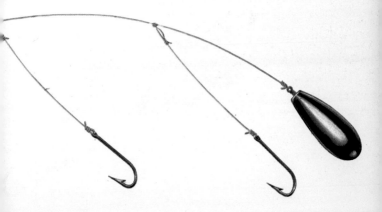

Tope often approach platform rocks.

FISHING FROM ROCK PLATFORMS

Fortunate is the angler whose coastline includes high rocks giving on to deep water, which can conveniently be fished from rock ledges above the water.

Not only mackerel, but much larger species, the most important of these being the tope, can be successfully tackled from rock ledges. Tope often find their way into small coves in pursuit of mackerel and flatfish. If you are lucky, you can spot them from the cliffs, on a still, clear day. They can be hooked by the use of somewhat specialized techniques.

Tackle is exactly the same as that recommended for bass fishing, with the exception of the reel, which should be a wide rather than a narrow-spooled multiplier, so that at least three hundred yards of eighteen-pound b.s. line can be carried on it. A four-foot trace of nylon-covered wire with a 6/0 hook is used, and the bait is a half-herring or mackerel. The lead runs freely on a boom – its weight will depend on the tidal conditions, but ideally a two-ounce or three-ounce bomb is the thing.

Because of its wind resistance, it is not easy to cast a half-herring a considerable distance to sea, but fortunately tope will often swim within close range. Once the cast is made, the rod is put down, and the reel must be out of gear and on check. The first indication of a take will often be a long, screaming run, followed by a pause, then another run. As in the case of boat fishing for tope, the strike should be made on the *second* run.

In this comparatively shallow water, i.e. under five fathoms, the tope will characteristically make long, repeated runs, and the fight is not usually a short one. If possible, the tope is tailed, but a gaff is sometimes required amongst rocks.

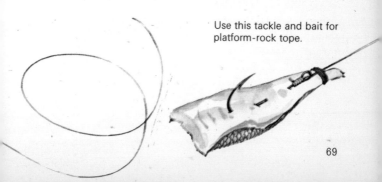

Use this tackle and bait for platform-rock tope.

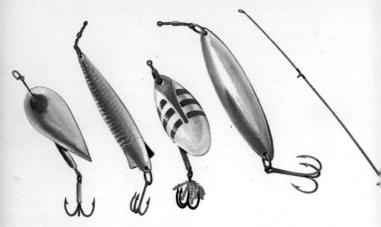

Spinning for Pollack

Another species which can be angled from rock ledges is the pollack. Such pollack are unlikely to be as large as their off-shore equivalents, but since the tackle can be scaled down a good deal, there is no lack of sport. Inshore pollack range from a pound or so to fish of seven or eight pounds. As they are taken in shallow water, the fight tends to be more exciting and prolonged than from bigger fish at greater depths.

The pollack is related to the cod, and to the coalfish, but there are marked points of distinction. The pollack has light-coloured smudges on its flanks. Unlike both the cod and the coalfish, it has no barbel beneath the chin. It is a fish of the eastern Atlantic as far north as Norway, and is not found in the Mediterranean. Pollack will eat small fishes, crustaceans and worms.

Best fishing times are in the early morning and late evening – indeed, the last hour of light is known as the 'pollack hour', or the 'suicide hour' amongst sea anglers. Small pollack will

Use a swivel to prevent kinking.

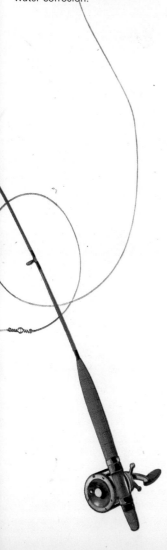

(*Left*) A selection of the lures used when spinning for pollack near rock ledges. (*Below*) A salmon rod is suitable — though it must be protected from salt-water corrosion.

sometimes take in the brightest part of the day, but they provide little sport. It is really hardly worth the angler's while to bother with them.

A salmon rod is an ideal weapon – though it should be carefully protected from the effects of salt-water corrosion. A fixed-spool reel can be used, though if the bottom is very foul (as it often is on pollack marks) a light multiplier carrying heavier line – up to fifteen pounds – is better. A swivel should be used above the lure to prevent kinking. Whether a lead is used depends on the depth of water, the speed of the current, and the weight of the lure. Wherever possible, try to do without a lead. It creates turbulence unattractive to fish, and may also foul the lure.

The heavy lures which cut out the need for a lead are big spoons (the long, slightly dished kind, are best), such as the ones shown opposite, German sprats and bar spoons. Rubber and plastic sand eels are sometimes used.

A long-handled landing net with plenty of capacity will be a must for the angler if the fish seem to be running more than three pounds or so in weight.

Float Fishing from Rocks

All three basic methods of sea fishing can be employed from the rocks: bottom fishing, as in the case of tope; spinning, as for pollack; and float fishing.

Float fishing will take a number of species, among them mackerel, wrasse, coalfish and pollack, and is perhaps the best way of taking bass from rocky shores.

The kind of rock platform that gives on to broken, stony, weedy ground is best for bass. The stones harbour much food. Crabs are the most important kind, but there are also prawns and small fish like gobies, rockling and blennies. These too are very attractive to bass. Another significant point is that this is the sort of ground favoured by very big bass. You are more likely to get a double-figure specimen in these surroundings than in any other.

Your beach-casting equipment can be used here, but ideally you should go much lighter. A carp rod such as freshwater fishermen use suits admirably, since heavy weights are not needed. Moreover, there is the advantage of more sporting fishing.

A carp rod and float give varied fishing from rocks.

A fixed-spool reel is also handy. It should be loaded with eleven-pound b.s. line – not less, for there are many hazards in such places, and it may be necessary to hold the fish hard at times.

A small pike float is best for this work – the plastic kind is suitable. As can be gathered from the illustration, this is large enough both to provide the required buoyancy and to be seen easily in various conditions.

Smaller floats can sometimes be used in very calm conditions, but a pike float is the best for all-round use. Depending on the bait, a single hook or a treble is used; a single is best for prawn or ragworm, a treble for soft or peeler crab. To keep the bait down in the water a spiral lead is used on the trace – a half-moon foldover in calm conditions.

The bait should be fished off the bottom – two-thirds of the depth is a handy rule. Take advantage of the tide so that the float washes in and out of gullies, and the bait covers as much ground as possible.

You will soon learn to manage this, and thus to offer your bait as close as possible to the fish.

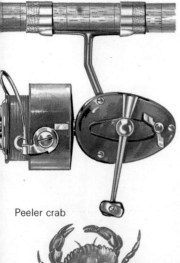

Peeler crab

Mackerel from Rock Platforms

In the months of high summer, when mackerel shoals approach very close inshore, splendid sport may be obtained by fishing for them from rock platforms. In July, August and early September, the best method is spinning, and full advantage can be taken of the sporting qualities of the species by using nothing heavier than a trout spinning rod and a fixed spool reel loaded with three-pound or four-pound b.s. line.

The lures that take mackerel are manifold. At this time of the year, mackerel will strike at any metallic bait, and if you are really hard pressed, tinfoil wrapped around the shank of the hook will take fish. But since tinfoil is somewhat inconvenient, more conventional lures which do not unwrap themselves from the hook and which are heavy enough to be cast long distances are best. Small, weighty silver spoons are best of all.

Bar spoons are good, but they are not so easily cast, and the angler limited as to position may find the shoals just out of reach when he uses them.

Mackerel shoals near rock
platforms give
splendid sport.

Attractive to mackerel, these lures are heavy enough for a long cast.

High water is often a good time to take mackerel by spinning from the rocks, and if this coincides with the last hour or two of light, so much the better.

Late in the season, when the mackerel shoals have broken up and many of the fish are already making their way into deeper water, big specimens may be taken by float-fishing a strip of mackerel flesh. These big fish – and they may weigh up to three pounds and more – seem reluctant to take a spinner, but will readily accept a natural bait.

Tackle can be as for float-fishing for bass – though go lighter if you possibly can.

Some people seem to undervalue the sporting possibilities of mackerel fishing. Perhaps they associate it chiefly with commercial methods, where the main aim must be to land a large haul of fish.

But it can give very good sport for rod-and-line anglers. At the right time of year, and perhaps at the right stage of the tide, the familiar mackerel is definitely amongst the fish that can provide very good angling from the rocks.

Wrasse Provide Sport

We have six species of wrasse in British waters, but five of them are inconsiderable from the angling point of view. This leaves us with the ballan wrasse, a fish that reaches the respectable weight of six or seven pounds in our coastal waters.

The ballan wrasse is brightly coloured, and shows considerable colour variation, but in general the fish is brownish or red, though the top of the back is dark, and the fins bluish. Small bright spots all over add further brightness. Still, these fish are by no means beautiful, with their rubbery projecting lips (well adapted to detaching limpets from rocks) and their heavy, stubby build. Nor are they good to eat.

But they do have the advantage of providing sport when not many other species will, typically on a blazing hot day when the sea is calm and the whole of marine life seems lethargic.

Limpets are a favourite food of
ballan wrasse.

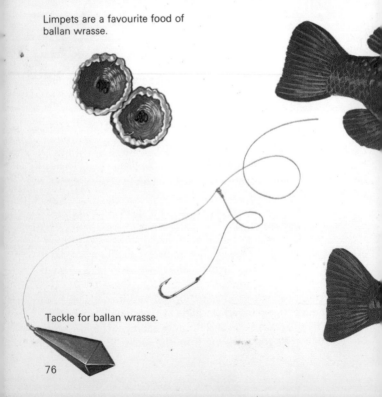

Tackle for ballan wrasse.

Another consideration is that they are lively fighters on light tackle, diving hard for the shelter of rock ledges the moment they are hooked. In my own view they have an important function in introducing young, would-be sea anglers to the sport. Wrasse are not hard to catch, and reach a fairly impressive size.

They are commonly taken close to the rocks, often directly before the angler, and float or bottom tackle can be used. If the latter, then the best plan is to allow the lead to tap the rock, then reel in a foot or so to avoid fouling. Since the fish can be allowed no line, a stiffish rod should be used. Practically any reel, loaded with twenty-pound b.s. monofilament, will be suitable.

The wrasse is also extremely obliging when it comes to bait. It is the only species I know of that will freely take limpets, gathered from the rocks and shelled on the spot.

Ballan wrasse detaching limpets from rock.

DEEP-SEA FISHING – PINNACLE ROCK

For all-round fishing in deep water offshore, there is no doubt at all that pinnacle rock in twenty fathoms or more provides the greatest sporting opportunities around the coasts of Europe. There are several reasons for this. The first is to be found in the unsuitability of such areas for commercial fishing. Again, pinnacle rock affords a refuge – from the commercial fisherman at any rate! – for many species, and it is amongst these that the angler with rod and line finds his opportunity.

Typically, pinnacle rock rises up from deep water and is in fact a complex of underwater fissures and crags that sometimes shoots ten fathoms or even more from the sea bed. Famous pinnacle rock marks include the Manacles on the south coast of Cornwall, and the Ling Rocks off Kinsale, in Co. Cork. There are also many others, less well known but just as prolific, off Northern Ireland, Scotland and West Wales. It is to be noted that for fishing purposes large wrecks create the same conditions as pinnacle rock, and are fished in very much the same way. The wrecks in Start Bay, Devon, are typical of these: probably the most famous of all is the *Lusitania* wreck off southern Ireland.

Chart produced by the echo-sounder. This one shows pinnacle rock and the position of a wreck.

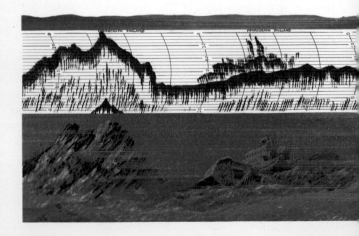

An echo-sounder, which tells the people in a boat what is to be found under the surface.

Pinnacle rock can be picked by several methods. A skipper with close knowledge of the area may be able to rely on visual bearings, though for these a reasonably clear day will be required. However, unless one's skipper can readily pick up a mark, specialized apparatus is needed. One useful device is the echo-sounder, which automatically records on a screen what is below the surface of the water. The pictures show the Ferrograph instrument and the chart it produces.

An echo-sounder apparatus is fitted in the boat and explores the seabed by sending sound-waves that 'bounce' back to the instrument in the boat. This records them on a chart.

Such a chart will show when the boat is over pinnacle rock. Thenceforward it is up to the skipper to maintain the craft in the best positions for fishing, despite the vagaries of wind, weather and tide.

In the picture the wreck of a large vessel is shown by the chart lying amongst the uneven contours of the pinnacle rock. The angler confirms that he has reached the desired area, and knows what fish to expect.

Pinnacle Rock for Variety

We have already had one indication of why pinnacle rock fishing is so good – the inability of commercial fishermen to approach these natural fortresses. But there are plenty of other good reasons as well. The peaks and valleys of rock provide a natural ambush ground for big fish that lie in wait for their prey. Smaller fish are attracted by the feed provided by weed growth, on the upper levels at least, and find shelter in the crannies.

Over the pinnacles swim shoals of red sea-bream and pollack, the exact depth depending on the time of day and the state of the tide. Closer to the rock itself, and along its slopes, will be ling, conger and coalfish, and possibly some of the bigger pollack. In deep gullies close to the bottom, where there are

In pinnacle rock, crannies form natural lairs for fish of many species.

sand or mud patches, very large common skate may be found, and on rare occasions a halibut that might weigh two hundred pounds or more. In the gullies also will be rock cod – the adjective does not imply a distinct species but a variety, often reddish-coloured, which does not seem to migrate in the manner of 'green' cod. Mako shark haunt pinnacle reefs, and modern theory insists they should be sought there.

Lesser fish – pouting and whiting, chiefly – will be present, and mackerel on the upper surface. Dogfish make an appearance sometimes, and tope may move in to attack the bream shoals, perhaps tearing a hooked fish from the angler's line.

Very interesting to the angler are the sporting problems that arise from pinnacle rock's variety of species.

Pinnacle Rock Conger and Ling

Pinnacle rock fishing gives the angler a wide choice of methods, depending on the kind of fish that he is seeking, and on the tidal conditions that prevail. Very often his choice is restricted by the unwillingness of the boatman to risk his anchor! That means drifting over the mark, and often loss of a good deal of tackle. To many anglers this will seem no great hardship – hooks and leads are not expensive items, and if a supply of spare traces is carried, not much time need be lost.

Two species which often fall to the angler who is drift fishing are ling and conger. Both are voracious predators that will rarely refuse a fresh bait fished close to them. Ling run up to forty pounds, conger much larger. In inshore fishing, conger are usually sought at night, but in deep water, of twenty-five fathoms and more, they will often feed through the daylight hours, so the angler must be ready for them.

The conger is a fierce, strong fish.

Rod and reel, with light harness.

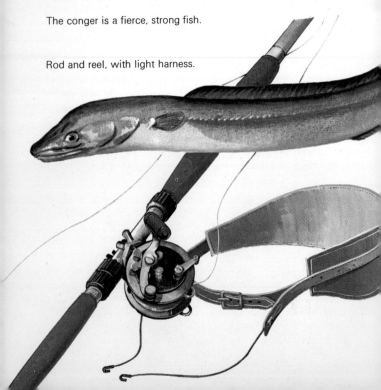

The ling — another strong fighter.

The tackle must therefore be rugged. A heavy boat-rod (test curve in the neighbourhood of seven pounds) should be used, and in conjunction with this a narrow-spooled, wide-diameter multiplying reel, like the Penn Super Mariner. The line (braided synthetic is best) should be not less than fifty-pound b.s. and many anglers will wish to go much stronger than this, for the strong, violent conger can reach a weight of a hundred pounds.

The end tackle should be very strong. A paternoster rig is best, since this is not so inclined to foul the bottom, and the links should be of wire or very heavy (sixty- to eighty-pound b.s.) monofilament nylon. Swivels used should be of large size, and thoroughly tested before they are used. Hooks (6/0 to 10/0) should be strong and sharp. The only weak part of the trace should be the attachment to the lead.

The best plan is to fit a 'rotten bottom' of cotton line or low breaking-strain monofilament for this link. Then a foul-up will result in the loss of the lead only.

Baits for Rock Bottom Fishing

Fishing on the drift is very much a matter of practice, of developing the 'feel' of the sea bed. The bait is slipped over the side and allowed to sink slowly through the water, the reel being checked with the thumb so that the trace streams out and does not foul on the way down. Letting out line in this way also means that the tap as the lead hits the bottom can be distinctly felt, and this is of the greatest importance, for as soon as contact is made, a fathom or so of line must be reeled up to prevent hooks and lead becoming fast to the rocks.

The two-hooked paternoster tackle should be baited with an oily-fish bait such as herring, mackerel or pilchard. In an emergency, a fillet of bream or of pollack can be used, but these are not first-class baits.

There are a number of ways in which the bait can be mounted, and each of them has its advocates amongst deep-sea fishermen. The simplest way is to use a whole single fillet taken from the side of the fish. The hook point should be passed through twice – at the thick or the thin end, according

Three ways (*right*) of mounting herring or mackerel as bait for big rock-fish. Note lashing on swallow-tail. (Lashing can also be used on a single fillet.)

Paternoster tackle (*far right*) with two hooks.

to your preference. The majority of anglers, myself included, bait through the thick end, but there is a school of thought which states that hooking through the thin end enhances the liveliness of the bait in the water.

Another method is the 'swallow-tail', in which two fillets are mounted, so that a fluttering effect is created. Whether you use one or two fillets, tying the top of the bait to the hook-shank with elasticated thread will ensure that it does not slip down and become a shapeless, un-attractive mass.

Finally, half a fish can be used, mounted as described for tope on page 69. This is perhaps not such an attractive bait as the others, for it does not exude blood and oil to the same extent.

Whichever style of baiting is adopted, it is worth while to change it at frequent intervals if no bite results. The attractiveness of a bait quickly declines when the blood and oil are washed out by the tide.

Fresh bait then becomes essential; obviously, the fish will not be interested in a dull bait, the appeal of which has been diminished.

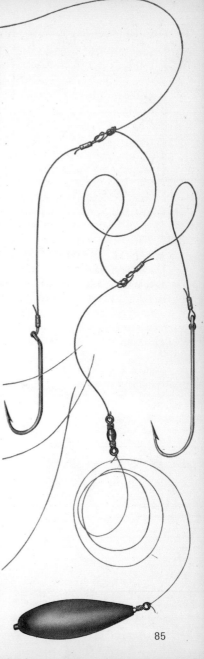

Quite wrong! If your rod rests on the gunwale, you cannot feel a bite.

Striking, Playing, Handling Big Rock Fish

Once the bait has been felt to reach the sea bed, the angler is ready to fish. He must never put the rod down in this kind of fishing; at worst he could forget to put the reel out of gear and lose all his tackle when a big fish hits; at best his tackle will be constantly hung up, since he is not there to feel for sudden elevations in the sea bottom, and to reel up out of the way.

Gaffing a conger. Note the boatman's glove.

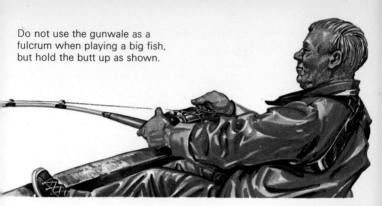

Do not use the gunwale as a fulcrum when playing a big fish, but hold the butt up as shown.

Moreover, he might miss bites. Characteristically, on the drift, a fish hits the bait quite hard. It may hook itself, but then again it may not. A positive strike is necessary, and the angler cannot achieve this when his rod is lying over the gunwale.

When large, powerful fish like ling and conger are concerned, a light harness is a great help, for much hauling work has to be done, and if the day is a good one, with plenty of fish, there is a serious danger of the angler becoming so fatigued as to lose interest in his sport. A harness puts the task on to the muscles best able to support it – those of the shoulders – and the angler can put much more pressure on the fish.

Typically, ling and conger put up a steady resistance, enlivened from time to time when the fish decides to put its head down and make for the bottom. The angler generally has warning of this, so that he is able to slacken off pressure. Fish should be given no leeway over pinnacle rock in the first stages of the fight, when there is a danger that they will regain a rock crevice from which you will not be able to remove them.

When you are playing a big fish, do not use the gunwale of the boat as the fulcrum of a lever, for the rod will break.

A gaff is essential in this fishing, and the boatman should be fully experienced in its use.

He must be able to use the gaff instantly and expertly to cope with the formidable problem of a large, fierce fish being taken into the boat.

87

Tackle for Lesser Rock Fish

In spite of the rugged nature of the sea bed, there are light fishing possibilities over pinnacle rock. These are provided by pollack and red sea bream, and there are many experienced fishermen who would argue that no finer sport exists.

When fishing with heavy gear and large baits, the fisherman may experience sometimes fierce, rattling bites although no fish is hooked. When the bait is retrieved, it will be found to be torn to shreds. This is the work of red sea bream (the most common of British sea breams, replaced in the English Channel by the black bream).

The bream found around the British coasts are in fact members of a large family, some of which belong to the Mediterranean. Colouring varies considerably between the different species, as does size, but the reddish tinge of some

Red sea bream. They go for bait
that is well off the bottom.

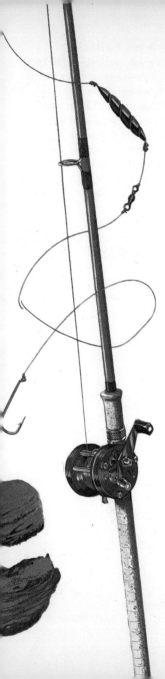

kinds is very distinctive. So is the shape, as shown in the picture below. Another point is that they have strong teeth.

Bream have very small mouths, though they are determined feeders, and it is no wonder that so few of them are hooked on conventional tackle. So a small, long-shanked hook (around Size 4 or 6) is used, on a trace that is as long as the angler can manage – about eight feet is a good length. The lead, a spiral or a Wye, is uptrace to this extent, and the whole thing is known as a flowing trace or drift-line.

Both rod and reel are very much lighter than the tackle used for ling and conger. This is because the bait is worked well off the bottom, and the quarry, though game, is much smaller. The rod should be as long as the angler can manage, and in big boats that are used for this work, he may even use a a ten-foot carp rod. A small multiplier such as the ABU 5000 is grand for this work, loaded with a line of about ten pounds breaking strain.

Light rod with flowing trace and multiplier. The hook is small because the red sea bream has a small mouth.

Baits for Bream (and sometimes Pollack!)

Undoubtedly the best bait for red sea bream is a strip of fresh mackerel cut very fine so that it will waver in the tide and attract fish. A very sharp knife is essential for the correct cutting of bait, so see that there is one in the boat before you begin fishing. The hook should be just nicked into the very end of the bait so that the mackerel strip will work properly.

The amount of lead will depend upon the run of the tide. You should use just enough to touch bottom some distance away from the boat, your line running out at a wide angle. Once contact with the bottom has been felt, begin to reel in,

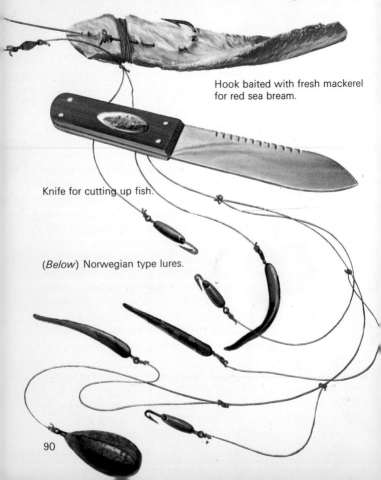

Hook baited with fresh mackerel for red sea bream.

Knife for cutting up fish.

(*Below*) Norwegian type lures.

Bream will sometimes go for feathers.

very slowly. Bream will first tap the bait, then rattle it more confidently. Keep reeling until the fish feels hooked, strike for good luck, and start to bring the fish in.

Bream fight all the way to the surface, indulging from time to time in vigorous dives that will test your light tackle to the utmost if you try to hold them. Since they have hard mouths, the hook-hold is not always good, and your boatman should be standing by with a large landing net. It is often fatal to let them splash at the surface, so keep your fish down until the net is ready.

Bream will often attach themselves to mackerel feathers and to Norwegian traces of the Fish-Fag type, but the above method is a good deal more satisfying than these, which involve heavier tackle and multiple catches.

Often whilst you are bream fishing, pollack will hit the bait. This is just a chance to be taken, and if you *do* hit a twelve- or fourteen-pounder, then you will certainly have a rare fight on your hands.

Pollack of the kind usually met under these conditions are a different proposition altogether. Bream of course can be very good sport, but if you happen to hook a big pollack the tussle is much more exciting and very much more worth while.

DEEP-SEA FISHING – BROKEN GROUND

Near pinnacle rock, there may be large areas of broken ground. These also are very prolific angling areas, though methods may be somewhat different from those adopted in rock fishing.

It might be worth saying a word here about the kind of boat that is best suited to these deep-water marks, which are often a long way offshore, especially since more and more anglers each year hire boats for holiday periods. The best kind of all is a broad-beamed fishing craft, quarter-decked at least, but ideally with some cabin space for shelter in bad weather.

'Broad-beamed' means wide in relation to the length. Any boat going to sea may roll, yaw and pitch at times, and may take spray aboard, but a suitable boat manned by experienced men is very safe and as comfortable as may be.

Speed is not essential, but the boat should have a good diesel engine with an alternative means of propulsion should it go wrong. There should be at least two men aboard as crew, to catch and cut bait, and to look after the angler's needs. (After all, he is paying a good deal for the privilege.) Gaffs and landing nets should be available, and wherever possible an echo-sounder. A thirty-five-footer, about right for this kind of work, should not take more than six anglers for bottom fishing, and three for shark fishing.

The echo-sounder can make all the difference to the success

(*Top right*) A thirty-foot off-shore fishing-boat, fitted with echo-sounder.

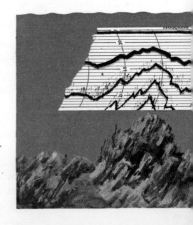

(*Right*) Echo-sounder chart of broken ground too rough for trawling.

of a fishing trip, revealing rocks and gullies and the kind of broken ground that we are discussing here. It excludes a great deal of guesswork and saves a lot of time.

The picture of broken ground given by a written-record echo-sounder is a profile of rugged weedy, stony ground that presents too much of a hazard to trawls to make it worth commercial fishing. It is therefore of considerable interest to anglers.

For amongst gullies and rocks and swirling currents, the fish swim undisturbed by the trawling of commercial fishermen.

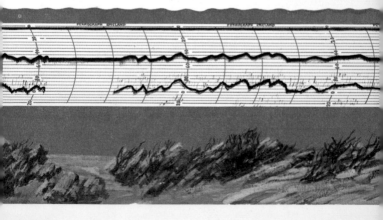

The Common Skate

The common skate is one of the largest fish found in European waters. Two other species, the long-nosed skate and the white skate, also reach large weights, but they are considerably rarer than the common skate, and, as angling methods are identical, there seems to be no point in differentiating between the fish here. A weight of a hundred pounds specimen is not remarkable, and many fish between 150 pounds and 200 pounds have been landed. Much bigger fish have been taken in trawls, and a possible maximum weight is 500 pounds.

Any fish of this size, is, of course, a predator (with the exception of the plankton-feeding basking shark), and the skate feeds on a variety of bottom-feeding fish – gurnard, flat-fish, smaller skate even. Not much that lives on the bottom comes amiss to it. It will even eat shrimps. On the other hand, the skate is no dashing pursuer of shoal fish. It flaps slowly along the ocean bed, and its method of attack is to flop down on its prey. Its teeth are designed for grinding rather than tearing, and if a big skate in the boat is alive, a seaboot that comes incautiously within range of it is liable to be crushed, and the owner's foot with it.

Skate are found in comparatively deep waters – specialist skate fishers should not seek them in much less than twenty fathoms, and they are found at much greater depths than this.

Skate have been taken in shallow water, but these tend to be the smaller ones. The really big fellows tend to lurk at greater

A large skate approaches its prey.

depths, and this presents its own problems, apart from the fact that the fish are larger and much heavier.

They are to be found on most types of ground, except for rock, but most typically they prefer broken ground. We have another helpful clue when we go out to angle for skate. They are often to be found in tide-races, or at the edge of them. Thus, broken ground of twenty fathoms or more, in or near a tide-race, is the classic ground for a skate.

Strong currents carry with them all sorts of items that form part of the skate's varied diet, and the big fish positions itself to catch them as they go by.

Certain areas produce big skate much more commonly than others: they are the western, southern and north-western coasts of Ireland, south Cornwall and the west coast of Scotland.

Altogether, the skate is quite a fish, not least because of its methods of resistance to the angler. Other fish may attempt to get free with determined darts, rushes and other fighting stratagems. The skate relies largely on its shape and of course often on its size.

And the unusual combination of factors – the habits of the skate and its size – make specialized methods necessary in angling for this big fish.

Baits and Tackle for Skate

Skate demand very heavy tackle. It is as simple as that. Not only can they reach enormous size, but their body shape is such that it puts up a massive resistance to the tide. Skate rarely run and exhaust themselves, like tope for example. In the early stages of the fight, they cling to the bottom, by pumping their 'wings'. Breaking the power of this suction requires a great deal of pressure that puts an almighty strain on both angler and tackle. Even when this bottom hold is broken, they have to be hauled to the surface.

Thus, the heaviest kind of boat-rod, with a roller-tip, must be pressed into service. The reel should not be smaller than a 4/0 multiplier (some anglers prefer a big, single-action reel), and it should be loaded with heavy line – fifty pounds b.s. minimum. This line should be braided synthetic, not monofilament. Mono line has too much stretch in it, enabling the fish to regain the bottom in the early, vital stages of the fight.

The trace should be a simple running ledger, with the short

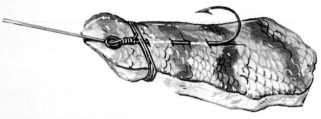

Mackerel lask and a flowing trace for skate.

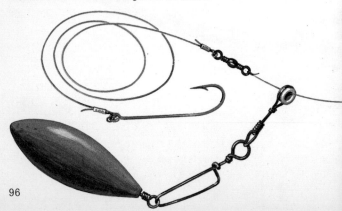

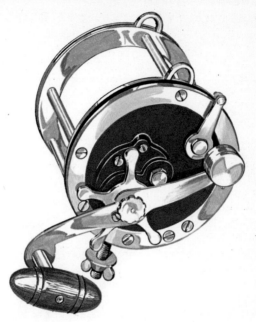

Heavy boat-rod and reel.

hook line (about one foot) of steel wire. It is a mistake to follow the practice of some anglers and incorporate a small hook link above the lead, to take any smaller fish that may come into the area. This leads to much reeling up and unhooking of gurnards, dogfish and so on, with a consequent lessening of the chances of catching the real quarry.

Do not disperse your effort. Remember that you are trying to catch skate, and do not try deliberately to mix this with fishing of some other kind.

The hook must be big – 9/0 or 10/0 – and well sharpened. The bait is a whole fillet of mackerel, cut very thick.

There is little room for doubt in tackle for skate. To repeat, it must be heavy and strong to cope with the size and weight of the fish and its habits.

Playing Large Skate

Many anglers, having caught a skate of more than a hundred pounds, are content to leave it at that. They have no wish to repeat the intense, back-breaking strain of hauling a great weight from a great depth – a weight, incidentally, that often comes to life and decides to head again for the bottom, stripping off in a few seconds line that has taken a long time to win back on to the reel. Sometimes you read in angling textbooks that skate come up like tombstones or dining tables. Do not believe it! Such remarks are made by angling authors who have never hauled big skate themselves. It is an exhausting business, taxing the angler's strength to the uttermost.

The angler should not be without a full shoulder harness and a belt to take the rod butt. Because I had forgotten mine, I once spent more than an hour landing a skate of just over 120 pounds, nearly all the work having to be done by my arm muscles, which ached for days afterwards.

Full harness means that 'pumping' the fish is made easier. This technique is the only practical way of landing a large skate. The rod-point is lowered towards the fish, the slack line is taken up, and the angler hauls upward until he is leaning right back. Then the rod-point is lowered quickly again, the slack line is taken in, and the process is repeated.

Later rather than sooner, a large white shape will show beneath the surface (skate come up belly first) and the last stage of the fight approaches. With the skate on the surface near the boat, the angler relaxes and eases the drag of his reel, just in case of accidents, for the boatman has now taken over, holding the trace in a gloved hand and slipping the gaff in.

Even under the best conditions, the end of the struggle is apt to leave the angler if not exhausted, at least convinced that it has been quite a battle. Often this feeling is justified, for if the skate is not an orthodox fighter, he presents a considerable angling problem and victory can be well worth while.

The pictures on the right show how the technique is applied in three separate stages. It is the only really suitable procedure for getting your skate to the surface. You are probably up against a large and heavy quarry, and it will need your skill and judgment, as well as all your strength, if you are to bring him within reach of the gaff.

Playing

Lifting

Pumping a skate

Winding up slack

The Huge Halibut

Halibut are an extremely rare catch in British waters, but this may not mean necessarily that they themselves are particularly rare. Halibut are enormous, predatory flatfish weighing between 50 pounds and 500 pounds. Almost all the specimens that have been caught by anglers around British coasts have weighed more than a hundred pounds. They are more active fish than skate, preferring a drifted bait to one which is stationary on the bottom, and as the majority of drifted baits are too small to interest them, it is no wonder that so few halibut are boated.

So if you are going for the big flatfish, bear in mind you must have an adequate bait.

Halibut are a cold-water species, and the specimens which turn up from time to time off southern Ireland are stragglers. For European anglers, the most likely places are near the Shet-

The huge halibut — a predatory flatfish — in a rock gulley.

lands, along the western coast of Norway, and off Iceland. Commercial long-line fishermen favour these areas.

Halibut are fished with long-lines – in other words, with baited hooks. The reason for this is that they favour low, rocky ground which cannot be worked with nets. Rock gullies in thirty fathoms of water and more are the places to search, and the bait must be a big one. My own single contact with a big halibut was made off Stavanger, Norway, when I was using a live three-pound cod as bait.

Tackle must be heavy: that recommended for skate will be suitable. We have little knowledge of halibut on rod and line, but halibut take very slowly. Do not strike too soon, or your chance will be lost.

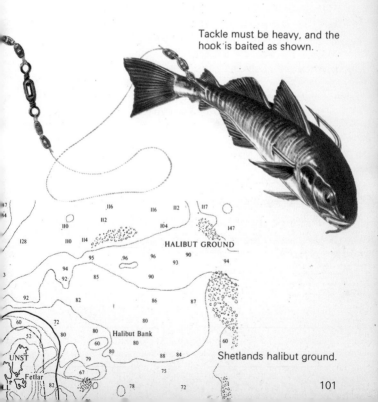

Tackle must be heavy, and the hook is baited as shown.

Shetlands halibut ground.

Cod Over Broken Ground

In Scotland and Ireland particularly, large cod in big shoals are sometimes to be found working over patchy, broken ground. Naturally, if he locates a shoal, the angler will seek to make the most of the opportunity. However, skill and judgment are both needed to get the best results. What is the best technique to adopt? In such circumstances, drifting is probably a better method than fishing to an anchor, as the fish may be split up, and the chances of anchoring on barren ground, especially when the area has been little fished, are somewhat daunting.

Paternoster tackle is used – two or three 6/0 hooks baited with single mackerel fillets. Tackle should be a medium boat-rod and a 4/0 reel loaded with thirty-pound b.s. line, the lead depending on the run of tide and the rate of the drift.

(*Above*) Feather lures for cod.
(*Below*) The Immelblinker lure appeals to cod.

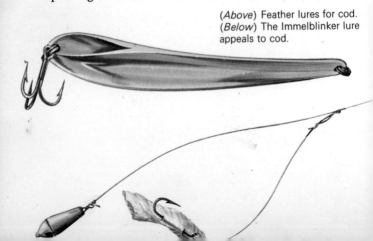

In this kind of fishing the anglers are seated along the length of the boat, as far apart as possible to obviate the risk of the lines fouling one another. It is important to distinguish between the drag of stones and weed on the bottom and the take of a fish. Curiously, cod will often take somewhat lightly on the drift on this kind of ground, and it is then necessary, by giving a little slack line, to drop the bait back to the fish, when he will take much more positively. Well-fed cod, particularly, will not bother to chase the bait.

When fish are coming thick and fast, when there is little time to cut and change the bait, or when, indeed, bait runs out, recourse may be had to a trace of feathered lures (not more than three) or heavy-duty Fish-Fag traces.

(*Above*) Norwegian fish-fag lures. (*Below*) Hooks baited for cod with mackerel fillets.

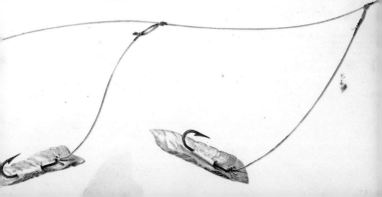

Coalfish

Another species that may be taken on the drift over broken ground is the coalfish. Coalfish somewhat resemble the cod, with a dark-green back, but there are no speckles on the body. A narrow line runs along the side; the barbel (below the chin) is very small.

Coalfish become increasingly abundant the farther north one goes. The smaller specimens, between a pound and three or four pounds, sometimes shoal in enormous numbers near the surface, almost in the way that mackerel do. When this happens they can be ring-netted in vast numbers. Incidentally, coalfish are used to make 'fish fingers' in many places.

But the angler will be chiefly interested in large coalfish, and to pursue these he must be willing to travel to the south-west of Ireland (the waters of Dingle yield some huge ones at times) to the north-west coast of Ireland, to Scotland, or to the Norwegian coast.

Coalfish are closely related to the pollack, which is not at all surprising, as pollack belong to the same order as the cod and the coalfish, but they differ very much in the way

Norwegians use chrome jigs like these for both coalfish and cod.

104

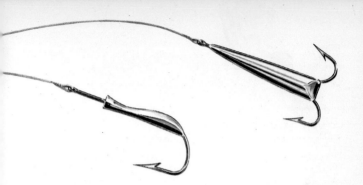

they feed. Pollack have a tendency to stay close to the reefs. Coalfish, on the other hand, are great wanderers, pursuing sprats and herrings at mid-water over all kinds of ground.

If you are trying with rod and line for coalfish, you should be ready to do as you would with other fish – consider their habits, especially their feeding, and the times and places to expect them.

The biggest specimens are likely to turn up in British and Irish waters in the autumn and winter months, and this is probably why they are not met more often, for in the areas in which they occur, little boat-fishing is done at these times of the year.

Tackle is as described for cod on the drift, with the proviso that coalfish, even more than cod, are likely to take an artificial bait. The Norwegians often fish them with murderous-looking 'jigs' (they take cod too in this way), but these are not likely to find much favour with British anglers.

Coalfish will sometimes shoal like mackerel.

Redfish and Tusk

Anglers visiting Norwegian waters (as more and more are doing) will quickly make the acquaintance of two species that are not found, or only rarely found, farther to the south. These are the redfish (or Norway haddock) and the tusk.

The redfish is quite a small fish, living in very deep water of fifty fathoms and more, but Norwegian anglers esteem it as a food fish. Redfish are to be found on rocky ground, and there is no need for any kind of specialist tackle, since they bite greedily when they are present and simply have to be reeled to the surface. The important thing is that the reel should hold plenty of line. Redfish are concentrated in certain spots, and you must get your marks just right. If no knock comes in the first moment or two, then it is time to shift ground.

You may be in the right area, but clearly you are not lucky enough to be in the right spot, so you must shift your position a little.

Tusk are more formidable fish, resembling our ling and having similar tastes. They are to be taken just off a rocky

Norwegian skerries are amongst the haunts of redfish and tusk.

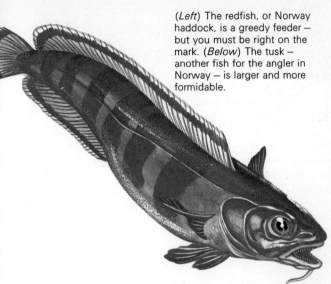

(*Left*) The redfish, or Norway haddock, is a greedy feeder — but you must be right on the mark. (*Below*) The tusk — another fish for the angler in Norway — is larger and more formidable.

bottom, so that drifting with herring bait is the most likely way to contact them. Like ling, they tend to be rather localized, but once you contact a 'hot' tusk spot, you may take several fish.

Tusk have fairly sharp teeth, so your hook links should be of wire to prevent their biting through.

DEEP-SEA FISHING – CLEAN AND MIXED GROUND

Generally speaking, ground that is regularly fished by trawlers is not of much interest to sea anglers. This is often the cause of disappointing sport when fishing trips are arranged, because commercial fishermen in all good faith have recommended certain areas as being full of fish.

Yet the presence of fish in what the trawl fisherman considers adequate numbers may mean something quite different to the angler with rod and line. Trawling is concerned with the area as a whole, and the total catch obtained from it. The angler, on the other hand, thinks in terms of a more limited area and of course a smaller total catch.

The point to be remembered is that a single sweep of a trawl can extend over several miles. The fish are not picked up steadily through the haul, but in patches. Thus a wide area may be 'good' from the trawler skipper's point of view, but

this is not much use to the sea angler, who must always have very precise marks.

In any case, fish that are much trawled over become disturbed and unwilling to feed – the ones that are not swept up in the net, that is. On the whole, broken and rocky ground is by far the best proposition for the sea fisherman. This is a comment of general application, and is not meant to exclude clean ground altogether. For clean ground with deep water over it may yield fish, if the echo-sounder is used to advantage. Shoals of fish tend to move in and out of areas like this (after all, there is little to keep them on clean ground), so that rarely is the water fished out. But what the echo-sounder does is to reveal the kind of place where fish may be found. The sea bed, even when it is of unbroken sand, is not absolutely flat. Gullies and trenches abound, and it is into these that fish move when the area is trawled. A careful survey with the echo-sounder will reveal such places, and these should be fished, at anchor.

They may enable the angler with rod and line to make a haul despite the fact that the area is trawled and that it is not from his point of view the most likely sort of ground

The picture below gives a good idea of a sea bed that in fact has quite enough irregularity to hold plenty of fish, and thus make angling worth while.

Echo-sounder in action, with chart showing gullies in sea-bottom.

Devon bays like this, and deeper waters
offshore, yield some really big whiting.

Whiting

As we saw earlier (page 28), there is an annual inshore movement of whiting in the autumn and winter, the fish coming into
shallow water, and qualifying, so to speak, for the attentions
of the close-range bay-fisher.

But during the summer, in deep water offshore, from twenty
fathoms and upwards, there is a resident population of big
whiting of three pounds and more that represent the best
chance the sea-angler is likely to have of contacting a real
monster of the species.

Such fish are often disregarded since there is bigger game
about, but a three-pound whiting is a real trophy, and should
never be undervalued. What is more, the fish are often present

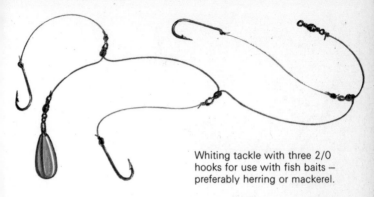

Whiting tackle with three 2/0 hooks for use with fish baits – preferably herring or mackerel.

in very big shoals, and bags of 3 cwt. or 4 cwt. can sometimes be made if the angler is single-minded enough.

The West Country is an excellent place for big whiting – the neighbourhood of Start Bay being particularly productive. Kinsale, Co. Cork, is noted for its very large whiting – and at times they can be caught three at a time. Scottish sea lochs have produced some enormous specimens, including a British record from Sheildag, Ross-shire.

Tackle need not be elaborate. Use a medium boat-rod, a multiplier with thirty-pound line on it and a three-hook paternoster is all that is required. If you are after big whiting, hooks somewhat larger than those sold in seaside tackle shops as 'whiting hooks' are needed – say, size 2/0's. Fish baits are best – especially strips of herring or mackerel – and should be from freshly caught fish.

Multiplier reel to take thirty-pound line.

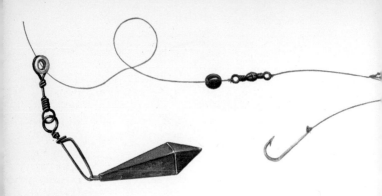

Pouting

Pouting (sometimes called 'pout' or 'pout-whiting') are almost universally distributed around the coasts of Northern Europe. The bigger specimens are to be found in the neighbourhood of reefs, but the small fish swarm over any kind of ground at most times of the year, meriting all the abuse they get from deep-sea anglers, who are after better game, and regard them as a bait-robbing nuisance.

Pouting, it will be seen, are by no means a highly-regarded sporting species, but they do have a number of functions which bring them within the orbit of the sea angler from time to time. They are obliging fish to begin with, which makes

(*Above, left*) Tackle and traces for pouting — unkindly regarded by some anglers as a bait-stealing nuisance. (*Below*) The larger pouting will swarm over offshore rocks.

them an ideal species for young anglers who are being introduced to the sport and need the encouragement of a large bag of fish in the early stages. They also make an excellent bait for congers — rather surprisingly so, since they are by no means an oily fish but a distinctly watery member of the cod family. (Despite this relationship pouting are fairly dark in colour, with a lighter under-side.)

On offshore reefs they may reach the respectable weight of three or four pounds: tubby, bronzed fish that bite like specimens three times their weight. Under these conditions they tend to pack over quite a limited area. For this reason you have to bear in mind that a pouting mark is often quite precise, and you need to be right on it to get the fish. Even a few yards can make a difference.

Considering what a nuisance they can be when they harass the bait of anglers who are after other fish, it is perhaps not surprising that pouting will take almost any bait known to the sea angler, but the bigger ones will prefer mackerel strips. Scraps of lugworm and fish will take the small inshore fish.

113

In Britain, Scottish sea lochs can yield good haddock catches.

Haddock

Haddock are most interesting members of the cod family – interesting for most British sea anglers, possibly, since they have made a remarkable reappearance in our inshore waters in the last few years. Previously, they were taken only rarely south of the Scottish coast, but they are now being taken in some quantity off the south coasts of England and Ireland – and good specimens at that, of up to eight pounds and more.

This is quite an interesting phenomenon, and a rather unexpected one, for haddock are really fish of the cooler waters, and as a rule they do not wander very far south.

There are several ways of telling the haddock from the cod, apart from the fact that cod run larger. The cod's tail is more or less straight; the haddock's is distinctly forked. The haddock has a black spot above the pectoral fin. The lateral line on the haddock is black, but the cod's lateral line is white. There are some other points of difference: the haddock has a smallish mouth, and the first dorsal fin is triangular.

Haddock prefer soft, oozy ground, and it is here that they should be sought. Northerly waters still produce them in greatest abundance. Scottish sea lochs, where there is a considerable depth of water – twenty fathoms or more – yield enormous catches of haddock at times, and so does the Norwegian coast. Like other shoaling members of the cod family, they can be taken in great quantities sometimes.

Drifting is a good way to take them, and a three-hook paternoster is the best tackle. Since they are not big fish, comparatively speaking, light tackle may be used. They fight well, and are a sporting proposition if allowed the chance. Baits which they respond to are soft ones like lugworm and mussel, although the larger specimens are quite capable of dealing with a substantial lask of mackerel. The bait should be kept as close to the bottom as possible. Haddock move in shoals, browsing, so to speak, on the mud, and rarely do they rise in the water.

In the Norwegian fiords, haddock are sometimes taken on small jigs fished in very deep water, as deep as seventy or eighty fathoms. That some large specimens take these baits, which are imitations of small fish, leads one to wonder whether the predatory tendencies of haddock have not been underestimated in the past. Possibly the growing number of fish available now will permit some experimentation along this new line of thought.

Echo-sounding of soft, deep-water haddock ground.

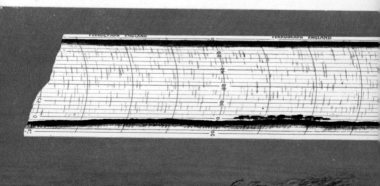

Gurnards

We have gurnards of three species in European waters, and they could not easily be mistaken for any other fish. The great wedge-shaped head tapering abruptly to the tail, the 'feelers' forward of the large pectoral fins, make the species easy to identify. It is not quite so easy, however, to distinguish between them. Anglers catching what they consider to be a record fish will do well to have the identification confirmed by a qualified person before making any claim.

Coloration is a rough-and-ready guide at best, but it is what most sea anglers go by. The grey gurnard, as its name suggests, is the least colourful of the three. Basically it is slate-coloured, but there are shadings of green and purple as well. Some grey gurnard have reddish tinges which make for confusion with the red and tub gurnards.

Grey gurnards — least colourful of their tribe.

The grey gurnard is the smallest of the British species, and is unlikely to exceed fourteen inches in length. Most specimens are a good deal smaller, which makes the species of very little angling interest. They are often caught, however, on baits meant for better fish, since they are of almost universal distribution in the summer months, and are taken even by the beach angler casting from the shore.

Of somewhat more interest is the red gurnard, a bottom-feeding species which nevertheless will rise in the water sometimes and take a mackerel spinner. A two-and-a-half pounder is an excellent specimen, and most red gurnard taken weigh a great deal less than this. Its brilliant red coloration makes it stand out from the less colourful grey and tub gurnards.

The tub gurnard itself is a much more considerable fish approaching double figures in weight. Tubs are caught over clean and mixed ground in a great variation of depths, from the shoreline to eighty fathoms and more. The most useful identification characteristic is that there is a brilliant blue border to its large pectoral fins.

The tub gurnard may reach a length of about two feet.

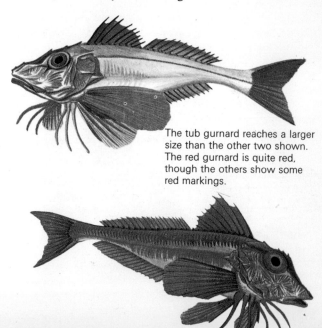

The tub gurnard reaches a larger size than the other two shown. The red gurnard is quite red, though the others show some red markings.

Dogfishes

The dogfishes are not the most popular of marine species amongst anglers. They are repellent in appearance and unpleasant to handle. They provide practically no sport when hooked. Nevertheless, they turn up, however unwelcome they may be, on many angling expeditions. They just cannot be ignored.

The dogfishes are in fact small sharks. The most common, and least attractive, is the lesser spotted dogfish, which is taken on clean and on patchy ground, and in both deep and shallow water. It is light brown, speckled with dark spots. The presence of one of these fish is indicated by a nagging pull-pull-pull at the line, and it is unlikely that it will leave the bait alone until it has thoroughly hooked itself. Unhooking it generally takes a long time. It is not very big, most specimens weighing two pounds or so.

A bigger version (up to twenty pounds or so) of this fish is the greater spotted dogfish, known in some angling circles as a bull huss. This also has dark spots, but the colour is rather more bluish. A heavy fish, it shows about as much animation as its lesser-spotted relative when hooked, but there are times when it puts up a sullen resistance. Both it and the lesser-spotted dogfish have nictitating eyelids – that is to say, they can wink! This is about their sole claim to fame.

The spur dogfish (called the piked dog sometimes) is rather livelier, but its appearance is generally greeted with even less

The spur dogfish is a small shark.

118

enthusiasm than that of either of the other two. It runs up to twelve pounds or so, and it is the only member of its family to operate in shoals. There are times when they invade a large area of sea in thousands, and then all other angling comes to a stop. It is utterly voracious and omnivorous, attacking wounded members of its own species. It will tear at any bait the angler cares to put down. The only time it is fished for deliberately is in competitions, where total weight counts. A wire trace must be used.

At other times it is just a nuisance, and, as can be gathered from the pictures, it would be hard to describe any of the dog-fish as attractive to look at.

The lesser (*above*) and greater spotted dogfishes. Note also the greater spotted dogfish's darker colour. (*Inset*): Greater Lesser.

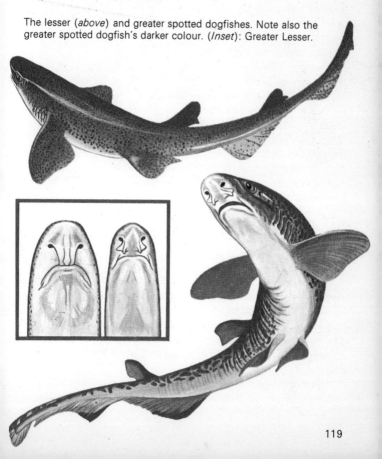

119

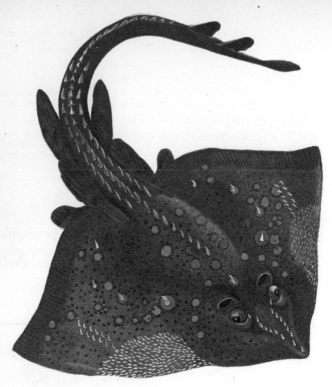

The thornback — for the angler the most important of the rays.

THE RAYS

Anglers distinguish between skate and rays, but there is no zoological distinction. All are species belonging to the family *rajiidae*, and all the angler is doing is separating the small species from the large.

Naturally enough, these fish are largely distinguished by the body shape (varying from roughly diamond-shaped to triangular); by the whip-like tail and often by pronounced markings.

The most important of these smaller 'rays' as far as the angler is concerned is the thornback, a species widely distributed in

Typical ray ground: sand shoals off the Essex coast.

European waters. The thornback runs from five pounds or so to a possible maximum of thirty-five to forty pounds. It carries distinctive spines on the back and running down along the tail. The colour could be called brownish, and on this background are many more or less circular markings of different sizes. It is a fairly important fish from the sporting point of view, and although it is no dashing fighter, it can give a respectable account of itself on light tackle, and is usually a welcome catch – not least because its wings, fried in butter, are quite delicious.

In late spring it is found in large numbers on sandbanks. Boat fishing is usual though the species is sometimes taken by the beach angler.

Thornbacks are particularly partial to soft crab bait and to sand eels, but they will take lugworm or ragworm or herring strip. Tackle need not be elaborate, though it is as well to keep it as light as possible. The boat should be at anchor and the bait fished right on the bottom. A running ledger is the best end-tackle, and the hooks should be 3/0 or 4/0 for this interesting fish with the slightly unusual appearance.

Cuckoo ray

Some Smaller Rays

There are a number of other rays that the angler is likely to meet, and telling them apart is really for experts. Some indication of species may be had by the outline and by the coloration, and by the area and depth in which the fish was taken. But correct identification of rays must really be a matter for the expert.

However, one can go some way towards identifying them by noting the characteristics of those commonly met with in British waters. (Overseas, especially in tropical waters, there are others with different characteristics. We are not concerned with them here.)

After the thornback, the blonde ray is one of the most widely distributed. Unlike the thornback, which often enters very shallow water, it is rarely found in depths of less than ten fathoms.

The blonde ray, as the name suggests, is light in colour. It carries on each wing three to five 'eye spots'. Around each of these is a ring of darker spots. (These eye spots, of course, are not organs of vision, which are obviously separate, but are camouflage markings.)

Found in company with the blonde ray, and very difficult to distinguish from it, is the homelyn, or spotted ray. A fairly

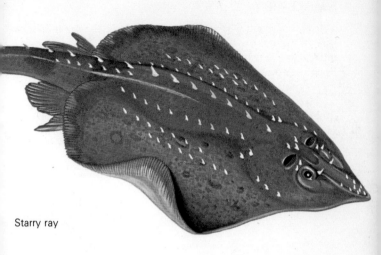

Starry ray

small fish, it is not often bigger than two feet or so.

The cuckoo ray is smaller still, and is found in quite shallow water. The sandy ray, a larger fish that might reach four feet, is not commonly taken by the angler, since it tends to be an offshore species inhabiting depths from forty fathoms upwards.

Colouring tends to be a greenish blue. You can recognize it by the distinctive dark eye mark on the wings – though immature specimens of other kinds of ray sometimes carry similar markings.

Spotted ray (homelyn)

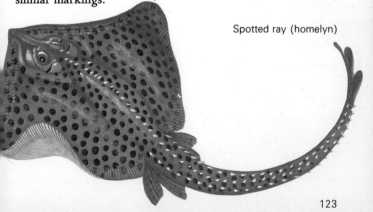

SMALL FRY

Whatever sporting species are the target of the sea angler, a host of small fry will inevitably be part of his fishing experience. Some of these fish, small as they are, will take his baited hook. Almost all of them are suitable for bait – often first-class bait – and a knowledge of their potentialities is always useful.

When feathering for mackerel, the greater sand eel is caught quite often. This silvery fish can be as much as a foot long: if you get one, remember that it makes an excellent bait for big pollack whilst alive, and ledgered dead on the bottom will take turbot and many other species.

The great tribe of gobies are more likely to be found in rock-

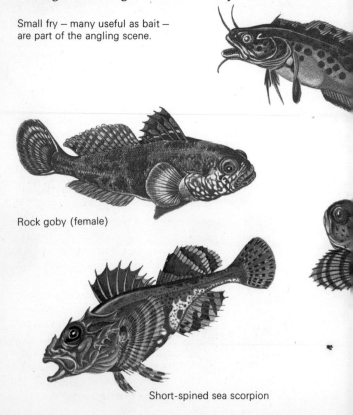

Small fry – many useful as bait – are part of the angling scene.

Rock goby (female)

Short-spined sea scorpion

Montagu's blenny

Three-bearded rockling

Shanny

pools, in company with blennies. We have at least ten species of goby and four of blennies. Gobies and blennies show considerable variation of form and colour. Many are hardly pleasing to look at. With float tackle over rocky ground, both species will serve as bait for bass.

Small rockling are found in the same sort of place. They (and the gunnel also) are sometimes known as 'butterfish'. Confusingly, south-coast anglers give the same name to a smooth-shelled cockle which is also a good bait.

A small enough hook in deep-sea fishing will sometimes take a fish that seems to be a small pouting, but on examination proves to lack the pouting's characteristic barbel. This is a poor-cod. Fished whole, of course, it can be very attractive to big conger eels. Fished alive on float tackle it has accounted for some very big bass.

Sometimes, whilst the angler is shore fishing, a more fearsome-looking specimen with large pectoral fins and an outsize head will take the soft-crab bait intended for bass. This is the sea-scorpion, which is not at all lethal, in spite of its appearance.

125

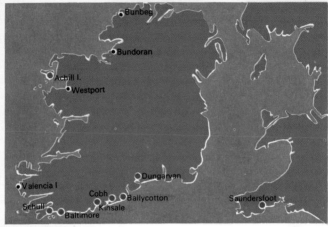

Shark-fishing centres in Ireland and South Wales.

Main centres
Other centres

BIG-GAME FISHING

Since the war, European sea anglers have become more and more interested in the possibilities of big-game fishing round their shores. It is especially true of Britain that possibilities not appreciated years ago are now being explored, and are revealing unexpected opportunities in home waters or not too far away. Previously, only the pre-war fishing for North Sea blue-fin tuna off the coast of Yorkshire had been attempted, and that, by 1945, had almost ceased, because of high costs and a growing scarcity of fish.

West Country and southern centres for shark fishing.

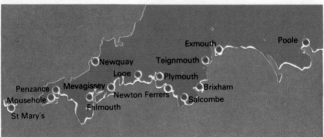

But now something of the potentiality of our coasts is beginning to be realized. It is obvious that Europe's sea-board will never provide the kind of big-game fishing that can be enjoyed in warmer waters, but there is enough to justify European sea anglers' dreams of marine monsters.

Sharks have proved to be much more numerous than was suspected at one time, and thriving sea-angling centres devoted to blue shark fishing in particular have been established in Cornwall, Wales and Ireland. Mako shark, which stand high in the hierarchy of big-game fish, have been shown to occur in waters from Cornwall south to Portugal, and there are porbeagle and thresher shark as well.

Broadbill swordfish occur in eastern Atlantic waters, and at the resort of Sezimbra, near Lisbon, numbers are taken each year. These fish probably range from south of the Irish coast down into the Mediterranean, and there is plenty of room for experimental fishing.

Big-Game Fishing — Atlantic Coast and Mediterranean.

Yellow-fin tuna occur in large shoals from Britanny south, and there is still a run of the giant blue-fin tuna in the North Sea and up the Norwegian coast, as well as through the Straits of Gibraltar into the Mediterranean. Oceanic bonito and albacore are two other species which occur. Persistent reports from the Algarve coast of Portugal indicate that marlin may be present as well in European waters – the most desirable big-game fish of all.

But European big-game angling is still in its infancy. A huge amount of pioneering remains to be done.

Fitted out for the job: a Looe shark boat.

Hunting the Blue Shark

The blue shark, though by no means the most formidable species in eastern Atlantic waters, remains the favourite game of most sea anglers with an inclination for big fish. The fish is unmistakably a shark. It is greeny-blue on top, and much lighter beneath. The head is the typical shark shape, set off by a pair of baleful eyes, and in front of the large pectoral fins are the characteristic gill slits.

'Blues' appear in British waters towards the end of June, and may be taken, e.g. with mackerel bait, until at least the end of September. On the Spanish Mediterranean coast the season may start in March, but it is over sooner. Most blues are not big fish – the average size is somewhere around fifty pounds – but there is always the chance of one much larger than this. The European record is over two hundred pounds.

A groin-protector for shark fishing.

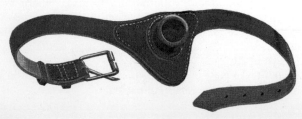

Shark rod with a 6/0 reel.

The fish sometimes come quite close inshore. It is not true that they are always at least ten miles out to sea, though of course they may be. The boat should be large enough to be seaworthy in open water. It must also be large enough to provide shelter and comfort for those on board. The number of anglers should not exceed three. The reasons for this will appear later.

The kind of gear which is hired to anglers by professional skippers is a good deal too heavy to give sport with the average fish.

Some specialist shark fishers now use a thirty-pound line, a 4/0 reel and a light rod. Beginners, shark fishing for the first time, are better off with a 6/0 reel and fifty-pound line. Heavy harness is not necessary (a butt-cup belt is sufficient). A very long, well-swivelled steel trace is used, and bait is a whole mackerel. But in addition to the conventional bait, another attraction is provided to entice the blue shark.

Mackerel as bait for blue shark.

'Rubby-Dubby' for Blue Sharks

Blue sharks are invariably fished from a drifting boat, and a special method is used to attract sharks from some distance away. Quantities of stale fish and blood are mashed together in a net bag until the mixture is fine enough for small particles of fish, as well as oil and blood, to be washed from it when the bag is suspended from the boat. Fishermen call it 'rubby-dubby'. As the drift continues, a 'slick' or trail develops. Sharks have a very acute sense of smell, and, having found the trail, they will follow it up until, eventually they come to the angler's bait.

As already indicated, shark fishing is not always a sport for one angler. Many would find it impracticable to pay the whole cost of hiring a boat and skipper, and perhaps gear as well, so two or three anglers may combine to form a party, and split the costs between them, agreeing to share the opportunities of sport as well as the expense.

The practice, where two or more anglers are fishing, is to

Rubby-dubby — a bag trailing a slick of fragments and an enticing smell — attracts the sharks.

have one bait swimming at ten fathoms, another at five, and a third close to the surface. Floats are used to suspend the baits, and these floats are fished at different distances from the boat, so that they will not foul one another.

Some skippers tend to overcrowd their boats with shark anglers, fishing as many as six baits. The end-result of this is often a complicated foul-up which spoils the fishing. Once a shark is hooked, incidentally, it is best for the other anglers to reel their baits. Even a hooked shark will sometimes take a second bait, and then there is trouble for all concerned.

On board should be two large, sharp gaffs, a hide glove for the boatman to use when grasping the trace, and a hammer for dispatching the fish. A live shark in the boat is highly dangerous.

Shark fishing in fact is largely a matter of teamwork, with the use of the right equipment and the right methods. With the boat the anglers hire the know-how and expertise of the boatman, and a good boatman is a great help.

Striking, Playing, Landing Blue Sharks

Shark fishing can afford thrills and action-packed minutes once the big fish has taken the bait, but the sea is vast, and the preliminaries will usually need a little time.

Most shark experts allow an hour or so for the 'rubby-dubby' trail to do its work, although runs will often come before this. In shark fishing the rod need not be held, but it should be placed in a secure position in the boat and the reel put out of gear and on check. If there is a strong drag with the tide, it may be necessary to have the reel *in* gear, but on light tension.

The take of a shark is usually very positive, the line running out fast to the accompanying music of the reel. But smaller specimens may take out line in short bursts, nodding the rod-top initially. Even when the first run is solid, it pays, as in the

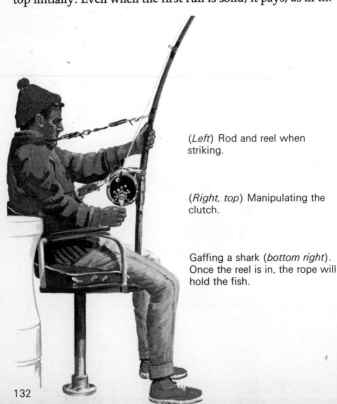

(*Left*) Rod and reel when striking.

(*Right, top*) Manipulating the clutch.

Gaffing a shark (*bottom right*). Once the reel is in, the rope will hold the fish.

case of tope, to wait for a second run to develop before striking.

The strike should be firm and positive, and the fish should be held for a few seconds to drive the hook well home.

What follows depends on the size of the shark and the gear you are using. On skipper's gear, it is merely a question of winching the fish to the side of the boat, unless it is a good one of a hundred pounds or so. On light gear, some lively play will ensue. The best policy is to humour the running fish until you can put more pressure on and begin to use pumping techniques.

Beware of the moment when the fish runs hard *towards* the boat, for the line could be bitten through.

When you have the fish at the side of the boat, ready for the boatman's gaff, ease your drag right off in case the gaffing fails and the fish makes a wild dash for freedom.

The Bigger Sharks

Much bigger sharks than blues swim in British waters, but they are not so often met. Perhaps this results from methods being geared to the capture of blues.

Thresher sharks are often seen, but rarely captured. The most remarkable feature of the thresher, of course, is its tail. The upper lobe of this is elongated to a relatively enormous length – sometimes greater than that of the rest of its body. With this it is said to capture the smaller fish that are its prey. It swims round them in ever diminishing circles, beating and splashing with its tail before it seizes them. Threshers are also said to hunt in pairs sometimes. This shark preys upon mackerel shoals. The main difficulty is for the angler to make his single mackerel stand out amongst thousands.

Porbeagles are mainly taken in the West Country and off Ireland, but they are probably present in numbers off the

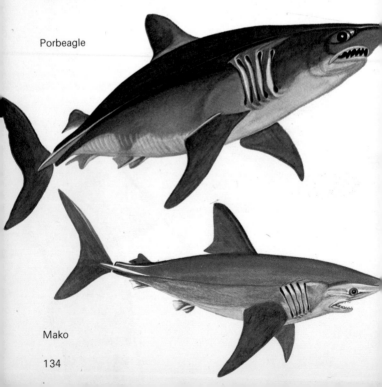

Porbeagle

Mako

Scottish coast as well. The most prolific area so far discovered is Galway Bay and north to the coast of Co. Mayo. The record fish of 365 pounds came from Achill Island in Co. Mayo.

The mako shark is the most interesting species of them all. Growing to an enormous size – over 1,000 pounds – it was only found to be present in British waters a few years ago. Earlier, mako had been wrongly identified as porbeagle. Nearly all the specimens so far taken have come from Cornish or Channel Islands waters. The first positively identified Irish mako was caught in 1965.

Mako can be called 'fast and ferocious'. They can catch fish that swim quite rapidly. When hooked they are strong fighters. They have been known to leap several feet out of the water in an effort to get free. All told, it is hardly surprising that they are renowned amongst large sporting fish.

The fight is likely to be arduous and may be long. There is always the risk of losing the fish. What a disappointment if this occurs through poor gear!

Thresher

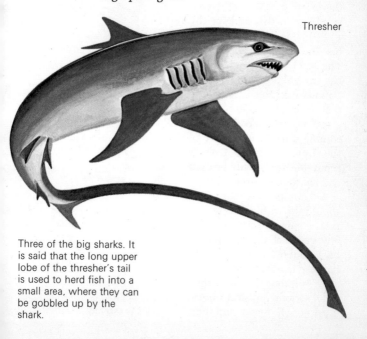

Three of the big sharks. It is said that the long upper lobe of the thresher's tail is used to herd fish into a small area, where they can be gobbled up by the shark.

Bait for Mako and Porbeagle

For big porbeagle and mako sharks, very heavy gear has to be used. Mako, especially, are very strong fish. A specimen hooked off the Manacles, Cornwall, in 1966 was played for seven hours before it broke away. The trace had frayed through.

Heavy rod and 9/0 reel.

Recommended tackle is therefore a 9/0 reel (some would go farther and specify a 12/0) loaded with 130-pound b.s. Dacron or Terylene line. The steel trace should be in the neighbourhood of 400 pounds b.s. This is to ensure that it is strong enough to stand up to a good deal of fraying during the course of the fight. A hook from a reputable firm should be used and sharpened carefully.

All links, swivels, etc. should be subjected to the most stringent tests. The last few yards of the line should be doubled. Full body-harness is absolutely necessary. Without it the angler risks serious physical injury.

Although mako and por-

In fishing for big sharks full body harness is essential.

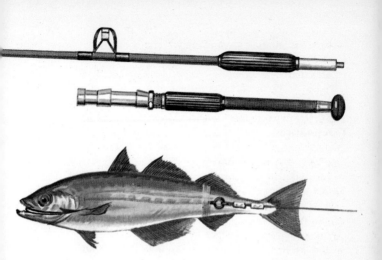

Ideal bait for really big sharks is a pollack or a cod of four or five pounds. If neither is available, mackerel can be used 'bunch of bananas' style.

beagle sharks chase mackerel shoals during the summer, it is probable that a large part of their diet consists of bigger fish. If only mackerel are available, then as many as half a dozen should be used, threaded on the hook and hanging down in 'bunch of bananas' style. The ideal, though, is a pollack or a cod of four or five pounds.

The pictures show the methods of mounting the baits suggested. Above is the hook with a lashing for a pollack or a cod. In the other picture is a 'cluster' of mackerel arranged so that they will be likely to attract the big fish as it cruises in search of a tasty morsel.

Mako and Porbeagle: New Ideas

The small band of sea anglers who have begun to specialize in the capture of big sharks have now concluded that mako in particular, and possibly porbeagles as well, do most of their feeding in the vicinity of pinnacle rock. A good proportion of the mako contacts made in Cornwall have been in the vicinity of the Manacles, and the Irish porbeagle were taken on similar ground around Moyteague Point, Achill Island.

Very long drifts, such as those carried out in blue shark fishing, may not be the answer, therefore, as far as mako and porbeagles are concerned. Dr O'Donel Brown, the Irishman who took the record porbeagle, fished to an anchor, and it may well be that anchor fishing will be proved better.

Moreover, there seems to be evidence that mako and porbeagle feed much deeper in the water than blues do, so that baits swum at depths of ten fathoms or less are not coming near enough to the fish. Further investigation into this aspect may prove rewarding.

Altogether, mako and porbeagle represent one of the greatest challenges to the modern sea angler, and if the problems they present are solved, then a considerable, and novel, sector of sport will have been opened up.

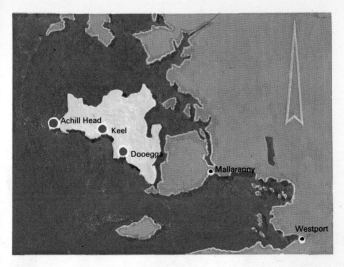

Achill Island centres for shark fishing.

The menacing Manacles. This notorious group of rocks lies off the south-eastern coast of Cornwall, a few miles north of the Lizard.

Playing Big Fish

It must be confessed that physical strength is a necessity for playing very big fish, i.e. of two hundred and fifty pounds and above. This is certainly true of European waters, where the sport is in its infancy. In the Caribbean, again, very fast sport-fishing launches are employed which transfer a great deal of the responsibility from the angler to the skipper, who virtually plays the fish with the boat. In some parts of Europe, boats tend to be slow and heavy, and skippers not very experienced in fishing of this type. To take an example, the big-game fisher-man in Portugal, anywhere outside the game-fishing centre of Sezimbra, is obliged to hire a commercial fishing boat and a skipper who will be a good seaman but quite uninstructed in big-game techniques.

Yet there are certain essentials that the angler should insist on. The first of these is a swivelled fighting chair in the stern of the boat from which he can play the fish. This should have a

(*Left*) The fighting chair and harness. (*Right*) The big fish brought to the boat for gaffing.

gimbal to take the butt of the rod, and the whole thing should be securely riveted to the deck.

The action of the fish can be very violent, especially if it is heavy. That is why a fighting chair firmly riveted to the deck is indispensable. It is essential for big-fish angling.

The boat should also be equipped with break-out-head gaffs. It is often impossible to hold a very heavy fish on gaffs attached to wooden or metal handles. With the break-out gaff, once the hook is in, the fish can be held on the rope. For landing a big fish, there should be an adequate crew – two, at least, besides the skipper.

Playing big sharks is a matter of coolness and stamina, with a determination to win line whenever possible and to ease the drag at the right moment. Mako, in particular, can be intimidating fish, leaping close to the boat. But experience has proved that fish up to a thousand pounds and more can be killed eventually.

BROADBILL SWORDFISH—PORTUGUESE STYLE

Broadbill swordfish are certainly present round European coasts from Ireland south, but it is only in Portugal that consistent captures are made. Commercial fishermen along the Portuguese coast take them on long-lines, and they are found in the Mediterranean as well. Some have been contacted by shark anglers fishing out of Gibraltar, though no satisfactory style of fishing has been evolved there as yet. Commercial craft, long-lining for porbeagle shark some forty miles south-west of the southern coast of Ireland, have entered Irish ports with broadbills aboard.

Swordfish of course are quite large, and on the upper part colouring is darkish. The distinctive bill – the sword – is flattish in section. It is believed that these fierce fighters use the sword to beat the fish on which they prey.

Occasional sightings of swordfish are made in British waters. One of the most recent records was of a fish of 130 pounds taken in the salmon nets in Bantry Bay, Co. Cork, in 1950. They can be mistaken for sharks in the water, since they have the habit of swimming with the dorsal fin and the tail (or the upper part of it) out of the water as sharks do.

Fishing for swordfish off the coast of Portugal.

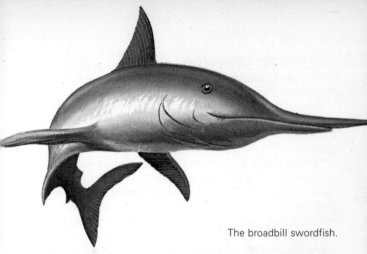

The broadbill swordfish.

The angler wishing to come to grips with this species, one of the most highly esteemed as a sport fish, would probably be best advised to go to Sezimbra, in Portugal, where a systematic approach is made to the sport. The best season is the autumn, especially in September, October and November.

Specially built big-game craft are available, but the actual hooking of the fish is done from a ten-foot dinghy – an *aiola* to use the name used by the Portuguese fishermen.

Live Bait for Swordfish

At Sezimbra, the method of fishing differs considerably from big-game fishing techniques at other centres.

However, it is the method approved by long local experience of the fish and of the prevailing conditions, and the angler who avails himself of local advice may reasonably expect good sport.

To begin with, a live bait is used, stationary on the bottom. The reason for this is that broadbills can best be located in these waters by looking for the commercial fishermen's long-lines. Just as the Yorkshire tuna fishermen of the 1930s sought out the herring drifters, in order to contact the big tuna that congregated around the nets when they were hauled, so the Portuguese realize that hooked fish on the long-lines are what draw the broadbills. Once again, it is a matter of realizing the feeding habits of the fish you are after.

The water is deep – sixty fathoms and more. The live bait, usually a Ray's bream, is let down, and the angler just sits and waits. The tackle is heavy – a 12/0 reel, 130-pound line – for the fish run large. Most specimens will be bigger than 200 pounds and there is always the possibility of much larger ones: the world's record stands at more than 900 pounds. Hence the tackle must be stout, and able to cope with large and lively fish.

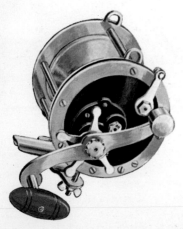

(*Left*) A 12/0 reel for broadbill swordfish.

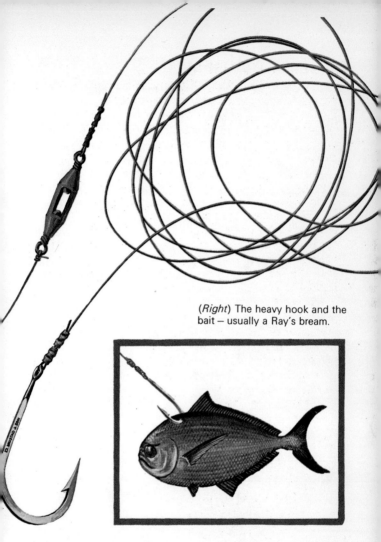

(*Right*) The heavy hook and the bait — usually a Ray's bream.

When a fish is hooked, what, in fact, plays it is the *aiola* (just as the dinghy played big blue fin tuna in the North Sea fishing). The aid of the parent boat is always available if required, as it is manoeuvrable and not far away.

If necessary – but especially in the case of an unusually large fish – the angler can go on board the larger craft to continue the battle, and of course with far better facilities.

CARIBBEAN GAMEFISH

A very different method of fishing for broadbills, as well as other big-game species, is adopted in Western Atlantic centres, where there has been a great deal more experience of this kind of fishing. This is the style that was evolved along the North American coast and in the Caribbean, as well as on the other side of the world, in New Zealand waters. It is undoubtedly the style which will be followed in European waters, once enough progress has been made and the fish have been proved to be there. Hence it is well worth describing, for the lessons that have been learned in those waters may well be applicable in other parts of the world where broadbills and some other large fighting fish are available.

The boats are often fine craft, with good cabin accommodation. Special care is taken to place the controls in handy positions for fishing.

The bait ready for trolling.

Boat with flying bridge.

To begin with, the boat is constantly on the move, under power. The bait is trolled, that is to say towed behind the boat, so that presumably it resembles a living, wounded fish swimming near the surface. Two baits are fished, and two extra ones, if necessary, from outrigger poles. These sometimes carry 'teasers' – large wooden plug baits which attract fish like broadbills. When they are seen to be interested, a natural bait is dropped back to the fish.

This method, and variations of it, is used to take game-fish species from amberjack to marlin. There are many refinements in equipment. One most useful addition to a game-fishing boat is a tuna tower, from which schools of fish can be sighted. Boats are linked by radio, so that a wide area can be searched, and productive areas made known. Then it does not take long for nearby anglers to converge, thanks to their powerful engines.

Trolling under power – a method adopted for big-game fish in Caribbean and other waters.

FISHING IN THE MEDITERRANEAN

Groupers form a large family of fishes which are found in warm waters of Europe, including the Mediterranean and the Atlantic coasts of Spain and Portugal. They reach a very large size – several hundreds of pounds in weight – but the majority of fish taken will be in the neighbourhood of sixty or seventy pounds.

Rod with pulley top ring.

They are fish of rock crannies, lying in wait for smaller species, so that fishing for them involves considerable difficulties. The bait must be kept near the bottom, and this means, in such terrain, that the angler has to endure many hang-ups and will lose much tackle.

The grouper can grow to a large size. It lies in wait in rock crannies.

Something of a speciality has been made of grouper fishing in the Straits of Gibraltar, and methods evolved there would probably be effective elsewhere.

Drifting is the basic technique, and a special three-hook tackle, like a very much enlarged version of the trout fisherman's Stewart tackle, is used. This is garnished with sardines – as many as half a dozen of them on occasion.

In the considerable depths

at which groupers are found – up to ninety fathoms are fished at Gibraltar – unless a special line is used, the line drifts away from the boat at too great an angle. To overcome this, a metal line has been developed (Monel Metal). This is fished on a Penn Super Mariner reel. The rod *must* have a pulley top ring.

Sea Breams of Warmer Waters

In Northern European waters, two common species of bream are present – the black and the red sea breams. But in the warmer waters of the Spanish and Portuguese Atlantic coasts, as well as within the Mediterranean, there swim a number of other species. Some of them reach a size undreamt of by anglers in more northerly seas.

The chief of these is the species known in Portuguese and Spanish as the *pargo*. In coloration it closely resembles the red sea bream, the most common British sea bream, but has a steeper forehead. It has been identified as *Pagellus erythrinis*. Summer visitors to the Algarve coast of Portugal may have seen these very big bream brought ashore by the boxful. Some specimens have been known to reach double figures.

Militating against this is the reluctance of many Southern European skippers to anchor over the rocky ground where

Light boat-rod and multiplier.

pargo are found. (They swim and feed very much in the manner described for red sea bream, page 88.) If the boat *were* brought to an anchor, then drift-line tactics could be employed and light tackle used. However, nearly all the available fishing is drifting over deep water. Off Gibraltar, however, where deep-sea angling is being developed on a considerable scale, anchoring tactics have been tried in recent seasons with some success.

From a boat in an anchored position, mackerel strip bait drifted on fifteen- to twenty-pound b.s. line would be entirely adequate for this type of angling. A light boat-rod, even a spinning-rod, could be used in conjunction with a multiplier. Orthodox heavy boat gear would have to be used from a boat on the drift, however.

Pargo — a sea bream that provides good sport off the coasts of Spain and Portugal.

The Formidable Moray

Moray eels have the reputation of being even fiercer than congers, and there are many well-authenticated cases of attacks being made on divers or on fishermen who have brought them to shore or into a boat. In all cases, though, attacks have been found to have been made only when the moray has been provoked.

Since the angler usually meets the moray in such circumstances, he should handle these creatures with the greatest caution. Growing to a possible length of ten feet, the moray can inflict formidable wounds.

Moray are almost always found inshore in rock crannies, and very heavy tackle is needed. Very often, a moray will lie

Heavy tackle for moray.

with the greater part of its body in a crevice, and strike at the bait in almost the manner of a snake. It is then very hard to dislodge the fish, if not, indeed, impossible.

A wire trace is, of course, a necessity, and 10/0 hooks are used. The trace is well swivelled. Braided synthetic line of a hundred pounds or more b.s., on a big multiplier or single-action reel, is fished in conjunction with a stiff hollow-glass rod of great strength. Fish or squid baits are used, the latter being most favoured in southern European waters.

Morays of different kinds, and growing to different sizes (sometimes very large) are found in many parts of the world, and they vary considerably in colour.

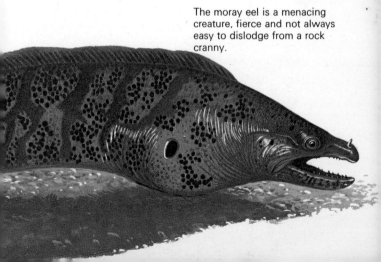

The moray eel is a menacing creature, fierce and not always easy to dislodge from a rock cranny.

Bonito and Albacore

Two species of bonito are of sporting importance in European waters, but they are mainly confined to the southern Atlantic coasts of Portugal and Spain, and to the Mediterranean. They wander into British waters only now and then.

The first is the oceanic or true bonito (*Katsuwonus pelamis*) and the second the belted bonito (*Sarda sarda*). Both species are related to the mackerel, but grow a good deal larger – the belted species may reach three feet. Both species are taken by trolling small artificial lures at a fairly high speed – the Japanese tuna feathers are particularly effective. Tackle can be light, and bonito, like other *Scombridae*, produce exciting sport. Larger fish may be expected in Atlantic waters than in the Mediterranean.

The albacore is another member of the *Scombridae* that may be taken by trolling methods in European waters. It reaches a

More power-boat trolling – this time in European waters.

large size: the record fish was almost seventy pounds, but average specimens are a good deal smaller than this, weighing twelve to fifteen pounds.

The fish resembles the tunny but the pectoral fin (the one on the side just behind the head) is much longer. The albacore is sometimes found in British waters, but in general prefers the Mediterranean or the warmer parts of the Atlantic.

As will be seen from the picture, a motor boat is used in this type of fishing as well. Some of these craft have the engine under the bridge-house, which contains the steering wheel and engine controls. These may be duplicated on the upper deck or 'flying deck' above the wheelhouse. Note the stout rods used, and the fighting chairs.

The movement of the boat enables it to cover a considerable area, and there is a good chance that the lure will interest one of these sporting fish.

Lures and hooks for bonito and albacore.

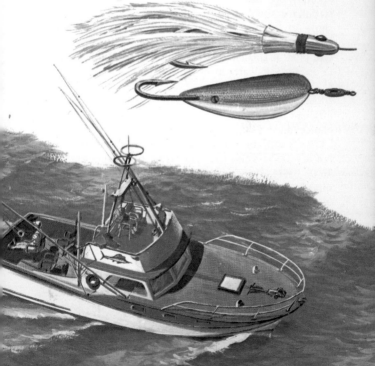

REELS, RODS AND LINES

Whilst it is realized that tastes, conditions and equipment available will show many variations, the following embodies useful general advice for the sea angler.

Reels
Sea anglers use all three basic designs, but it is helpful to keep in mind some of the features of each.

Single Action Reel This is the least popular, and is seen less and less often. It has a rotating drum, and is not geared. It is pleasant to use for casting out from the shore, but its range is limited. A single-action reel of large diameter (around seven and a half inches), so long as it is robustly built of alloy that will resist corrosion, is very good for dealing with a heavy skate being fished from a boat.

Fixed Spool Reel This is a type in which the line coils off a stationary spool. It is commonly used for casting from the shore. With it one can throw a bait moderately well out into the surf, though one cannot achieve the distances that a multiplier will give. A smaller fixed-spool reel, though, is the best kind to use for salt-water lures that weigh less than an ounce.

Multiplier Reel Of this reel one can say that it is the most efficient for both shore and offshore fishing, and that it is the choice of most expert anglers.

The small, narrow-drummed models are ideal for surf-casting for bass and cod. The larger sizes, from 4/0 right up to 16/0, cover everything from light boat-fishing to catching blue-fin tunny. The small, very free-running spool of the multiplier is driven through a series of gears. The gearing can be completely disengaged for casting with a free spool, and a drag arrangement can be set so that fast-running fish can take off line without the handles revolving (a considerable hazard to the angler's knuckles with a single-action reel).

Rods
Although split-cane rods are still made for sea use, they are becoming much less common. Fibreglass is now preferred –

hollow for the best. Solid fibreglass is suitable for very heavy boat-fishing models.

For shore-casting, a double-tapered or tip-actioned model of between eleven feet and thirteen feet (depending on the angler's build and height) should be specified. A six-foot or seven-foot rod is most convenient for boat fishing. The strength of the rod will depend on tidal conditions and depths to be encountered, and upon the probable size of the quarry.

Lines

Here also there is a fair choice, but it can be narrowed down for practical purposes.

For spinning and shore casting, use monofilament nylon, renewing it each season.

For boat work in normal conditions, a braided synthetic line of Terylene or Dacron is best. (Anglers usually call it 'braid' for short.)

In very fierce tidal conditions, 'Monel' (alloy) line should be used, and for this the rod must have a roller tip-ring.

Admiralty Charts

It was announced in April 1968 that Admiralty charts, prepared under the direction of the Hydrographer of the Navy, would be converted from fathoms to metres. In view of the great deal of work involved, the process was expected to take some time, but it would proceed as rapidly as practicable.

Record Weights

Species weight records given in this book may have been replaced by other records set up since compilation.

Acknowledgments

The charts on pages 18 and 26 are based upon sections of Admiralty Chart No. 1478 (St Gowan's Hd. to St David's Hd.), and are reproduced with the sanction of the Controller of HM Stationery Office, and of the Hydrographer of the Navy.

The chart on page 101 is based on Chart No. 70A (Fishing Chart North Sea) published by Imray, Laurie, Norie and Wilson, St Ives, Huntingdon.

INDEX

OTHER TITLES
IN THE SERIES